T0176864

ARTIFICIAL INTELLIGENCE IN PRACTICE

ARTIFICIAL INTELLIGENCE IN PRACTICE

HOW 50 SUCCESSFUL COMPANIES USED ARTIFICIAL INTELLIGENCE TO SOLVE PROBLEMS

BERNARD MARR

with MATT WARD

WILEY

This edition first published 2019
© 2019 Bernard Marr

Registered office
John Wiley & Sons Ltd, The Atrium, Southern Gate, Chichester, West Sussex, PO19 8SQ, United
Kingdom

For details of our global editorial offices, for customer services and for information about how to apply
for permission to reuse the copyright material in this book please see our website at www.wiley.com.

The right of the author to be identified as the author of this work has been asserted in accordance with
the Copyright, Designs and Patents Act 1988.

Wiley publishes in a variety of print and electronic formats and by print-on-demand. Some material
included with standard print versions of this book may not be included in ebooks or in
print-on-demand. If this book refers to media such as a CD or DVD that is not included in the version
you purchased, you may download this material at http://booksupport.wiley.com. For more
information about Wiley products, visit www.wiley.com.

Designations used by companies to distinguish their products are often claimed as trademarks. All
brand names and product names used in this book are trade names, service marks, trademarks or
registered trademarks of their respective owners. The publisher is not associated with any product or
vendor mentioned in this book.

Limit of Liability/Disclaimer of Warranty: While the publisher and author have used their best efforts
in preparing this book, they make no representations or warranties with respect to the accuracy or
completeness of the contents of this book and specifically disclaim any implied warranties of
merchantability or fitness for a particular purpose. It is sold on the understanding that the publisher is
not engaged in rendering professional services and neither the publisher nor the author shall be liable
for damages arising herefrom. If professional advice or other expert assistance is required, the services
of a competent professional should be sought.

A catalogue record for this book is available from the Library of Congress.

A catalogue record for this book is available from the British Library.

ISBN 978-1-119-54821-8 ISBN 978-1-119-54896-6 (ePDF)
ISBN 978-1-119-54898-0 (ePub)

10 9 8 7 6 5 4 3 2
Cover Design: Wiley
Cover Image: © mattjeacock / iStock.com

Set in 11/14pt MinionPro Light by Aptara, New Delhi, India
Printed in Great Britain by TJ International Ltd, Padstow, Cornwall, UK

CONTENTS

CONTENTS

Part 2 Retail, Consumer Goods and Food and Beverage Companies

Part 3 Media, Entertainment and Telecom Companies

CONTENTS

Part 4 Services, Financial and Healthcare Companies

CONTENTS

INTRODUCTION

One thing is very clear, artificial intelligence (AI) is going to change our world forever. And the change is likely to be more profound than most people realize today. No matter what job you are in, no matter what business or industry you work in, AI is going to augment, if not completely transform, it.

AI is giving machines the power to see, hear, taste, smell, touch, talk, walk, fly and learn. This in turn means businesses can develop completely new ways to interact with their customers, offer them much more intelligent products and service experiences, automate processes and boost business success.

Having said that, we also know there is a massive amount of hype and confusion about AI. Some see it as the ultimate threat to our civilization, while others believe AI is the savior that's going to solve humanity's biggest challenges, from tackling climate change to curing cancer. The aim of this book is to cut through the hype and scare-mongering, and provide a cutting-edge picture of how AI is actually being used by businesses today.

By sharing some of the latest and most innovative real world use cases from across many industries, we hope to demystify AI while at the same time inspiring you to see the immense opportunities AI is offering. We have written this book for anyone who would like to better understand AI and have therefore tried hard to keep the technical details to a level anyone can understand. At the same time, we have attempted to include just enough techie stuff to make it informative for people who already work in the field of AI.

In this book, you will of course gain insights into how some of the AI giants such as Google, Facebook, Alibaba, Baidu, Microsoft, Amazon and Tencent use it, but you will also learn how many traditional incumbent companies across most industries as well as innovative start-ups use AI. Our hope is that this will provide a realistic picture of the current state of the art: where the AI trailblazers are rolling full steam ahead, leaving many traditional businesses behind in the starting blocks; where traditional businesses are working hard at reinventing themselves and using AI to stay competitive; and where start-ups are using AI to challenge both the AI trailblazers and traditional businesses.

The Most Powerful Technology Of Mankind

AI is the most powerful technology available to mankind today and the biggest mistake anyone can make is to ignore it. Leaders of nations and businesses alike are seeing both the magnitude of opportunities AI brings and the risks of being left behind in the AI goldrush.

In the United States, the White House has released numerous policy documents that emphasize the strategic significance of AI. In 2016, under President Barack Obama, the White House issued the first report "Preparing for the Future of Artificial Intelligence",[1] which laid the foundation for a US AI strategy. In 2018, under Donald Trump, following an AI summit at the White House, the administration issued "Artificial Intelligence for the American People"[2] in which President Trump states: "We're on the verge of new technological revolutions that could improve virtually every aspect of our lives, create vast new wealth for American workers and families, and open up bold, new frontiers in science, medicine, and communication." The goal of the US Administration is to maintain American leadership in AI by accelerating AI research and deployment, and by training the future American workforce to take full advantage of the benefits of AI.[3]

Russia's President Putin said: "Artificial intelligence is the future, not only for Russia, but for all humankind. [...] Whoever becomes the leader in this sphere will become the ruler of the world."[4] China has arguably developed the most ambitious plan to make use of AI with a goal of becoming the world leader in AI by 2030.[5] In Europe, the European Commission released its AI strategy in 2018, in which it states: "Like the steam engine or electricity in the past, AI is transforming our world, our society and our industry. Growth in computing power, availability of data and progress in algorithms have turned AI into one of the most strategic technologies of the 21st century. The stakes could not be higher. The way we approach AI will define the world we live in."[6]

Business leaders agree. Amazon CEO Jeff Bezos believes we have entered the "golden age" of AI that allows us to solve problems that once were the realm of sci-fi.[7] Google co-founder Sergey Brin said: "The new spring in AI is the most significant development in computing in my lifetime"[8] and Microsoft CEO Satya Nadella calls AI the "defining technology of our times".[9] The founder and executive chairman of the World Economic Forum, Klaus Schwab, together with many others, believes that AI (especially when combined with all other technological innovations) has triggered a fourth industrial revolution that is going to transform all parts of business and society.[10]

What's Artificial Intelligence? The Rise Of Deep Machine Learning

AI is nothing new and nothing magical. The first developments in AI date back to the 1950s. AI refers to the ability of computer systems or machines to display intelligent behavior that allows them to act and learn autonomously. In its most basic form, AI takes data, applies some calculation rules (or algorithms) to the data and then makes decisions or predicts outcomes.

For example, the data could be images of handwritten words, letters or numbers. The algorithm would be a computer program written by a human that contains rules such as the common shapes of each letter and spacing between words. This then allows a computer to analyze scanned images of handwritten text, apply the rules and make predictions about which letters, numbers and words it contains, enabling machines to recognize handwriting. This type of AI has been used, for example, by the US Postal Services to automatically read addresses on letters from as early as 1997. For narrow applications this kind of AI worked well.

This rule-based AI runs into difficulties when tasks are more complex or when we humans can't easily explain the rules and therefore can't program them into algorithms. Speaking our language, walking around and recognizing a friend in a crowd are all examples of skills that we have acquired through experience but for which we can't easily explain the rules.

We have learned those skills via a network of neurons in our brain that have been programmed to, for example, recognize a face by looking at the face from lots of different angles over a period of time, or we have learned how to walk and talk through trial and error. In modern AI, we basically replicate this process using artificial neural networks and instead of having humans programming the rules, we let the machines create the rules by themselves, similarly to how our brain learns from experience. We refer to this as machine learning.

In machine learning, we train AI with data by, for example, feeding it thousands of images that either contain human faces or don't contain human faces. The computer then takes in the information and creates its own algorithm either completely independently (unsupervised machine learning) or with help from humans (supervised or semi-supervised machine learning). When machine learning uses multiple layers of artificial neural networks to learn from training data (which makes them more powerful), we refer to it as deep learning.

Deep learning has given us many of the recent advances in AI, such as the ability for computers to see and recognize what or who is in an image or in a video (machine vision). Or it has given machines the ability to understand and reproduce written text or spoken words, which we call natural language processing and see in website chatbots or home smart speakers like Amazon's Echo.

There are two key reasons why deep learning is thriving today:

1. We have data: Data is the raw material that is fuelling AI and in today's big data world we are generating more data than ever before. The digitization of our world means that almost everything we do leaves a data trail and we are increasingly surrounded by smart devices that collect and transmit data. This is causing exponential growth in the volume and types of data we can now use to train AI.

2. We have computing power: We now have the ability to store and process vast amounts of data. Breakthroughs in cloud computing allow businesses to cheaply store almost unlimited volumes of data and use distributed computing to analyze big data in near real time. What's more, advances in chip technology mean AI computations can now be performed on devices such as smartphones or other smart connected devices. We refer to this as edge computing on Internet of Things devices.

We humans continuously learn and improve through experience. This "learning by doing" approach can now also be replicated by machine learning algorithms via reinforcement learning. Similarly to how toddlers learn to walk by adjusting actions based on the outcomes they experience, such as taking a smaller step if the previous broad step made them fall, AI uses reinforcement learning algorithms to determine the ideal behavior based upon feedback from the environment. Reinforcement learning gives machines (for example, robots) the ability to walk, drive or fly autonomously. Many leading-edge applications of machine learning combine deep and reinforcement learning techniques.

If you would like to learn more about any of these fascinating topics, head to www.bernardmarr.com where you can find hundreds of articles and videos explaining and discussing everything you need to know about AI and machine learning.

Artificial Intelligence Opportunities In Business

There are three key use cases for AI in business, which can overlap to some degree, but help to segment the opportunities. Businesses can use AI to: (1) change the way they understand and interact with customers, (2) offer more intelligent products and services, and (3) improve and automate business processes.

Customers: AI can help businesses better understand who their customers are, predict what products or services customers are likely to want, predict market trends and demands and provide more personalized interactions with customers. In this book, we will look at companies like Stitch Fix and Facebook, which use AI to really get to know their customers.

Products and services: AI can help businesses create more intelligent products and services to offer to their customers. Customers want more intelligent products such as smarter phones, smarter cars and smarter home devices. In this book, we will look at how Apple, Samsung and car companies such as Tesla and Volvo use AI to create smarter products and we explore how others like Spotify, Disney or Uber use AI to deliver more intelligent services to their customers.

Automate processes: AI can improve and help automate business processes. In this book, we will look at examples such as JD.com that is using autonomous drones, automated fulfilment centers and delivery robots to transform its retail operations. We will also look at how AI can automate medical diagnosis in the Infervision and Elsevier case studies, and even the pizza quality checks at Domino's.

The Strategic Use Of Artificial Intelligence In Business

Exploring the applications of AI in any business will often lead to a business model refresh or even a complete transformation of the business approach. It is important that companies don't use AI to automate and improve a business model that is no longer relevant during the fourth industrial revolution.

The starting point for any use of AI should be an AI and data strategy that identifies the biggest strategic opportunities and threats for any business and then pinpoints the most impactful applications. It is important to recognize that simply experimenting with AI around the edges is not going to deliver the necessary effects on business success.

Artificial Intelligence In Practice

In this book, you will find 50 company use cases and within them even more leading-edge examples of how these companies have used AI in practice to solve real world problems. We have divided the book into five parts.

Part 1 contains case studies from the AI trailblazers. These tech companies are the ones that have grabbed hold of the AI opportunities and are running with them to transform industries and deliver mouth-watering business results. Most of them have made innovative applications of AI part of all aspects of their business and therefore provide great insights into the art of the possible.

We could have segmented the remaining case studies in different ways, by AI application or by industry. Based on the feedback we received, we opted for the following industry segmentations.

In Part 2 we look at retail, consumer goods and food and beverage companies. In Part 3 we explore how media, entertainment and tele-com companies use AI. Part 4 looks at the services sector, including financial services and healthcare. Finally, in Part 5 we look at manu-facturing, automotive, aerospace and industry 4.0 case studies.

You can simply read this book cover to cover or dip in and out to explore the case studies or industries you are most interested in. We hope you will enjoy it!

Notes

1. Preparing for the Future of Artificial Intelligence, Executive Office of the President, National Science and Technology Council, National Science and Technology Council Committee on Technology, October 2016: https://obamawhitehouse.archives.gov/sites/default/files/whitehouse_files/microsites/ostp/NSTC/preparing_for_the_future_of_ai.pdf
2. Artificial Intelligence for the American People, The White House: https://www.whitehouse.gov/briefings-statements/artificial-intelligence-american-people/
3. Summary of the 2018 White House Summit on Artificial Intelligence for American Industry, The White House Office of Science and Tech-nology Policy 10 May 2018: https://www.whitehouse.gov/wp-content/uploads/2018/05/Summary-Report-of-White-House-AI-Summit.pdf
4. "Whoever leads in AI will rule the world": Putin to Russian children on Knowledge Day: https://www.rt.com/news/401731-ai-rule-world-putin/
5. A Next Generation Artificial Intelligence Development Plan: http://www.gov.cn/zhengce/content/2017-07/20/content_5211996.htm and Three-Year Action Plan to Promote the Development of New-Generation Artificial Intelligence Industry: http://www.miit.gov.cn/n1146295/n1652858/n1652930/n3757016/c5960820/content.html
6. Communication from the Commission to the European Parliament, the European Council, the Council, the European Economic and

Social Committee and the Committee of the Regions, Artificial Intelligence for Europe, Brussels 2018: https://ec.europa.eu/digital-single-market/en/news/communication-artificial-intelligence-europe

7. A.I. is in a "golden age" and solving problems that were once in the realm of sci-fi, Jeff Bezos says, CNBC: https://www.cnbc.com/2017/05/08/amazon-jeff-bezos-artificial-intelligence-ai-golden-age.html

8. Google's Sergey Brin warns of the threat from AI in today's "technology renaissance": https://www.theverge.com/2018/4/28/17295064/google-ai-threat-sergey-brin-founders-letter-technology-renaissance

9. Microsoft CEO Satya Nadella on the rise of A.I.: "The future we will invent is a choice we make": https://www.cnbc.com/2018/05/24/microsoft-ceo-satya-nadella-on-the-rise-of-a-i-the-future-we-will-invent-is-a-choice-we-make.html

10. The Fourth Industrial Revolution: what it means, how to respond, Klaus Schwab, World Economic Forum: https://www.weforum.org/agenda/2016/01/the-fourth-industrial-revolution-what-it-means-and-how-to-respond/

Part 1
ARTIFICIAL INTELLIGENCE TRAILBLAZERS

1
ALIBABA

Using Artificial Intelligence To Power The Retail And Business-To-Business Services Of The Future

Alibaba Group is a Chinese multinational conglomerate that operates the world's largest e-commerce network through its web portals, which include Alibaba.com, Taobao, Tmall and Ali Express. With global sales that dwarf those of Amazon and eBay combined,[1] the business took what it learned from building a global online retail platform and has applied it to enterprises in just about every area of business and technology. Alibaba's success in delivering e-commerce and retail services, electronic payment, as well as business-to-business cloud services, has earned it a market cap in excess of US$500 billion.

Its customers use artificial intelligence (AI) tools to help them find what they want when they shop at its online portals, and as one of the world's largest cloud computing providers it also licenses platforms, tools and cloud services to other businesses to help them leverage AI.

Beyond that, Alibaba is rolling out AI across the wider society, with projects involving turning entire cities into "smart cities". They are also planning on revolutionizing China's (and perhaps the world's) agricultural industries to ease the burden of feeding a growing population.

How Does Alibaba Use Artificial Intelligence?

The Chinese government has strongly supported efforts by businesses to adopt AI, clearly believing that it has enormous potential for driving economic growth. Its goal is to foster a $1 trillion industry and be the world leader in AI by 2030.[2]

This, combined with the fact that the country's enormous population gives companies access to huge amounts of data on customers' lives, makes the country a fertile ground for AI development.

Alibaba's e-commerce portals use sophisticated AI to choose which items to display to customers when they visit and search for products they want to buy. It does this by building a custom page view for every visitor, aimed at showing them items they will be interested in, at prices that seem right.

By monitoring customer actions – whether they make a purchase, browse to a different item or leave the site – it learns in real time to make adjustments to these page views to increase the probability of the visit ending in a purchase.

To train its e-commerce portals to show visitors pages that are likely to result in a sale, Alibaba has deployed a form of semi-supervised learning known as reinforcement learning on its Taobao portal.[3]

Because collecting enough user data to train unsupervised learning algorithms from real-time customer actions would take a long time, and involve real business risks, a virtual Taobao was built, with customer behavior simulated from hundreds of thousands of hours' worth of historical customer data.

This mass of data meant that it was possible for the algorithms to be exposed to a far wider range of customer behaviors, in a far shorter time span.

Alibaba also has its own AI-powered chatbot – Dian Xiaomi – that answers more than 350 million customer enquiries a day, successfully understanding more than 90% of them. These tools are necessary to help it deal with the huge spikes generated by special occasions such as the Alibaba-created "Singles' Day" shopping event.[4]

Automated Sales Copy

With millions of different items on sale across its sites, Alibaba has invested in automated content generation to ease the burden of writing descriptions for everything it sells. The tools are also available to third-party sellers on its platforms.

Its AI copywriter uses natural language processing algorithms running on deep learning neural networks to produce 20,000 lines of copy in a second.[5]

Traditionally, sales copywriters have had to spend hours researching keywords and click-through rates to understand what is likely to make a customer click their link in a page of product search results. The AI copywriter allows Alibaba and others selling through its platforms to do it at the click of a button.

This is done by creating multiple versions of adverts and running them through algorithms trained on customer behavior data. The system works out which combination of words is most likely to result in customer clicks, and uses them to create its copy.

Cloud Services

Just like Amazon and Google, Alibaba offers artificially intelligent services through the cloud to its business customers. Its cloud service business is the largest of all the Chinese tech giants.[6]

Alibaba's AI offering is called Machine Learning Platform for AI, which offers solutions for businesses wanting to take advantage of cognitive computing functions such as natural language processing and computer vision, without the upfront costs of directly investing in infrastructure.

Alibaba's natural language processing technology was the first in the world to beat a Stanford University test designed to assess whether a machine can beat a human at reading comprehension.

In 2018, its deep neural network language processing technology passed the 100,000 question test with a score of 82.44 – narrowly beating the human score of 82.3.[7]

Smart Cities

Alibaba has developed a suite of cloud-based AI tools designed to carry out essential jobs like managing traffic flow, lighting and waste collection in cities where infrastructure is connected through smart online technology.

Alibaba City Brain already tracks and manages traffic flow on every street of Hangzhou, a city with a population of 9.5 million. The system is reported to have reduced traffic jams by 15%[8] and is soon expected to be deployed in Kuala Lumpur, Malaysia.

City Brain monitors the flow of traffic and builds up models that it can use to predict when congestion is likely to occur. When it recognizes signs that there is a high probability of this happening, it can alter traffic light patterns to speed up or control the flow of traffic, so jams are less likely to form.

Alibaba's AI also powers the smart ticket kiosks at Shanghai's subway stations. The kiosks give customers route information when asked, and check customer identification using facial recognition technology.[9]

Smart Farming

Alibaba has developed an AI system for monitoring farm herds, crops and orchards.

As the world's biggest supplier and consumer of pork, Chinese pig farmers have access to technology that records activity and health levels of herds, automating decision making over when to increase feed or provide animals with more exercise.[10]

Facing the challenge of feeding an ever-growing population, the system allows farmers to optimize breeding rates by raising a healthier herd and reducing newborn death rates. The system also has applications in crop growing and land management.

Academy For Discovery, Adventure, Momentum And Outlook

Alibaba's AI strategy is based around distributing its cutting-edge machine learning and deep learning solutions to businesses and customers through its cloud services.

Its business AI platform is delivered through its Alibaba Cloud subsidiary, which operates 18 global data centers. These host the hardware that powers the AI algorithms and data processing technology, which is provided as a service.

In 2017 it announced it would invest $15 billion over the next three years, expanding its global network of AI research and development facilities.

It calls this program the Academy for Discovery, Adventure, Momentum and Outlook – DAMO – and will involve recruiting 100 researchers for its labs in Beijing and Hangzhou, China, and San

Mateo and Bellevue in the United States, as well as others in Moscow, Tel Aviv and Singapore.[11]

Research at the labs will focus on machine learning, natural language processing, Internet of Things, human/machine interaction and quantum computing.

Key Challenges, Learning Points And Takeaways

- Alibaba is China's biggest investor in research and development, which has given it a strong start in the race to become the world leader in AI.

- Its model for rolling out AI to millions of customers and businesses is to deploy its services through the cloud. This cuts customer risk and infrastructure cost, while giving Alibaba access to valuable data about how its customers behave.

- By applying technology designed to drive sales at its retail portals to other problems in business and society, it identifies new use cases for AI, within and outside its established business operations.

Notes

1. Institutional Investor, Ali Baba vs The World: https://www.institutionalinvestor.com/article/b1505pjf8xsy75/alibaba-vs-the-world
2. CNBC, China is determined to steal A.I. crown from US and nothing, not even a trade war, will stop it: https://www.cnbc.com/2018/05/04/china-aims-to-steal-us-a-i-crown-and-not-even-trade-war-will-stop-it.html
3. Virtual-Taobao: Virtualizing Real-world Online Retail Environment for Reinforcement Learning: https://arxiv.org/abs/1805.10000
4. SCMP, Alibaba lets AI, robots and drones do the heavy lifting on Singles' Day: https://www.scmp.com/tech/innovation/article/2119359/alibaba-lets-ai-robots-and-drones-do-heavy-lifting-singles-day

5. BBC, The world's most prolific writer is a Chinese algorithm: http://www.bbc.com/future/story/20180829-the-worlds-most-prolific-writer-is-a-chinese-algorithm
6. Data Center News, Alibaba gives AWS, Microsoft and Google a run for their cloud money: https://datacenternews.asia/story/alibaba-gives-aws-microsoft-and-google-run-their-cloud-money/
7. Bloomberg, Alibaba's AI Outguns Humans in Reading Test: https://www.bloomberg.com/news/articles/2018-01-15/alibaba-s-ai-outgunned-humans-in-key-stanford-reading-test
8. Wired, In China, Alibaba's data-hungry AI is controlling (and watching) cities: https://www.wired.co.uk/article/alibaba-city-brain-artificial-intelligence-china-kuala-lumpur
9. Technology Review, Inside the Chinese lab that plans to rewire the world with AI: https://www.technologyreview.com/s/610219/inside-the-chinese-lab-that-plans-to-rewire-the-world-with-ai/
10. Financial Times, Alibaba brings artificial intelligence to the barnyard: https://www.ft.com/content/320fb98a-69f4-11e8-b6eb-4acfcfb08c11
11. CNBC, Alibaba says it will invest more than $15 billion over three years in global research program: https://www.cnbc.com/2017/10/11/alibaba-says-will-pour-15-billion-into-global-research-program.html

2
ALPHABET AND GOOGLE

Maximizing The Potential Of Artificial Intelligence

Alphabet is a US-based multinational internet services, technology and life-sciences conglomerate. Its businesses include internet-search giant Google, life-sciences company Verily, self-driving technology company Waymo, smart home device company Nest, artificial intelligence (AI) company Deep Mind, among others.

In his founder's letter in 2017, Sergey Brin, the president of Alphabet, wrote: "The new spring in artificial intelligence is the most significant development in computing in my lifetime."[1] Given that this includes the arrival of the internet, it's no small statement.

Alphabet understands the potential of AI and is set to use it across its businesses, from improving internet searches, to self-driving cars, automated homes, intelligent virtual assistants, language translation and life-saving medical science.

How Does Alphabet Use Artificial Intelligence?

Smarter Searching

Google's search engine – the most widely used in the world – is peppered with AI. Whether you use its text, voice or image search capabilities, every query is now (since at least the introduction of its Rankbrain feature in 2015) processed by smart, self-teaching systems.[2]

Text and voice search both employ natural language processing, so the algorithms attempt to understand how each word you enter as part of a search query relates to every other word it is used with, rather than just what each word means individually. This is semantic analysis, the key to natural language processing.

Google Image search uses computer vision to recognize the content of image data cataloged by Google, and classifies it so users can search for it using text or voice. Deep learning algorithms allow it to become increasingly good at recognizing and labelling different elements contained in pictures. The greater the variety of images it is exposed to, the better it becomes at knowing what they are.

Once Google's AI has processed your query and decided what it thinks you really want, it matches it against its directory of online content – web pages, images, videos and documents. These have also been processed by machine learning systems.

The systems are trained to sort, rank and filter all of the content in its directory. Content is assessed for how frequently cited (linked) it is, the accuracy of information it contains, the possibility that the information might be spam or advertising, and whether it is likely to be illegal or copyright infringing.

This means a simple Google search involves a great deal of complex, blisteringly fast AI calculations. Building systems capable of processing billions of calculations every day from all around the world is what has made Alphabet and Google a genuine giant in the field of AI (as well as one of the richest companies in the world).

Google uses AI for many of its other core applications, including security measures, which keep Gmail accounts secure, and adwords, which allow businesses to pay for their ads to appear in searches of customers who may be interested.

Artificial Intelligence Personal Assistants

AI personal assistants using voice technology have been around for a few years now and Google Home, Amazon Alexa and Apple Siri are familiar to most of us.

Although these first implementations of natural language processing into consumer devices seem impressive compared to what was possible just a few years ago, anyone who has used one will know they have limitations. They can respond well to basic, relatively short sentences and commands, but try talking to them like you would an actual human and things start to unravel.

This is because, in human terms, they are still very much infants. Put simply, they haven't had enough data yet. This is quickly changing, and Google's Duplex tech is leading the charge.

Duplex is able to hold far more natural, less jilted conversations. This is because it is specifically trained for particular situations, and its algorithms exclusively specialize in gathering data that is relevant to those situations. An example used by Google to showcase its ability features Duplex making a call to book an appointment at a hair salon on behalf of its user.[3] In these relatively controlled and constrained use cases, it comes very close to appearing perfectly human.

One trick used by Google's engineers to get the machine to sound more human was to incorporate imprecise elements of our speech patterns. For example, it will utter an "umm", an "aah" or an "mh-hmm" in places where it might seem natural for a human to do so.

Language Translation

Thanks to machine learning, if you can teach a computer to speak one language, it can teach itself to speak any language. That's the principle behind Google's language translation service, which uses deep learning to break languages down to their fundamental building blocks.

Google Translate uses deep neural networks to constantly refine its algorithms as its users expose it to more languages. This means it becomes increasingly efficient at accurate translations. Google has even built the feature into its Google Assistant-powered Pixel Bud headphones, meaning users can get near real-time translations directly through their headsets.[4]

Self-Driving Cars

Alphabet's autonomous vehicle division, Waymo, has one of the most mature self-driving car platforms in the world, having recently become the first to make rides available commercially.[5]

Alphabet has gone down the road of developing its own vehicles, which are so automated they don't even include steering wheels or any driver controls. Designed for a new age of urban motoring where car ownership is often expensive and inconvenient, Waymo's service is aimed at the ride-sharing networks, which it predicts will make up transport networks in smart cities of the near future.

Captioning Millions Of Videos

Google also uses machine learning natural language algorithms to automatically create subtitles for the hard of hearing (or those who value peace and quiet) for videos on its YouTube video-streaming service.

As well as speech, the system uses deep neural networks to identify ambient sounds, including applause, music and laughter and automatically displays text telling the viewer what sounds are occurring.[6]

Diagnosing Disease

Alphabet's AI (specifically deep learning) technology has also been extensively deployed in the medical field. One recent breakthrough involves diagnosing eye conditions. For this, it applies learning algorithms to 3D infrared scans of eyeballs known as optical coherence tomography scans.[7]

The system relies on two deep learning algorithms, one of which builds up a detailed map of the eye's structure and learns about what is normal and what could be indicative of a problem such as age-related macular degeneration. The other makes diagnoses based on medical data and provides medical professionals with assistance in diagnosing and treating the illness.

Google Brain

Google's AI research division is known as Google Brain. It was formed by Google's Jeff Dean and Greg Corrado along with Andrew Ng of Stanford University in 2011, and their work has established them as pioneers of the current wave of practical AI technology.

Google Brain realized that the vast, super-fast storage networks it had built up, as well as the huge amount of data flowing through the internet (and therefore its servers), were the keys to unlocking the usefulness of machine learning and deep learning.

Since it was established, this group has been responsible for developing many of the core technologies, such as computer vision and natural language processing, driving the current wave of AI adoption in business.[8]

Deep Mind

Another key weapon in Alphabet's AI arsenal is Deep Mind, which it acquired in 2014. The UK start-up specialized in building neural net "simulations" of the brain, which it trained to play games. The focus on gameplay enabled Deep Mind's researchers to study the way the brain tackles various cognitive problems, and use the data to build machines that attempted to tackle problems in the same way. The technology made headlines in 2016 when it powered the first computer that was able to beat a professional human Go Player.[9]

Today AI technology developed by Deep Mind powers a number of Alphabet's smart applications, including optimizing the efficiency of cooling machinery in its data centers, and managing battery life on mobile devices running the Android operating system. It's also the brains behind the eye imagery in the healthcare application mentioned above.

Key Challenges, Learning Points And Takeaways

- Alphabet and Google clearly believe that AI is the launchpad that will drive the next wave of transformative computer technology.

- As well as this, they believe the societal impact of this next wave will be even greater than that of previous waves – including the development of the internet.

- Having more data than anyone else is a key advantage, which has enabled Alphabet to continue to develop first-in-class services – from search, to ad serving, language translation, speech processing, smart homes and autonomous driving.

- Having the infrastructure in place to move that data around, and the processing power to query and access it at super-fast speeds required to power its search engine, enabled Google to apply the same infrastructure to AI applications.

- Where Alphabet has seen breakthrough development in leading edge AI, such as deep learning, by research groups and start-ups, Google has used its financial resources to bring it on board and add their expertise to its own.

Notes

1. Alphabet, 2017 Founder's Letter: https://abc.xyz/investor/founders-letters/2017/index.html
2. Search Engine Land, FAQ: All about the Google RankBrain algorithm: https://searchengineland.com/faq-all-about-the-new-google-rankbrain-algorithm-234440
3. Google, Google Duplex: An AI System for Accomplishing Real-World Tasks Over the Phone: https://ai.googleblog.com/2018/05/duplex-ai-system-for-natural-conversation.html
4. The Verge, The Pixel Buds' translation feature is coming to all headphones with Google Assistant: https://www.theverge.com/circuitbreaker/2018/10/15/17978298/pixel-buds-google-translate-google-assistant-headphones
5. Financial Times, Alphabet's Waymo begins charging passengers for self-driving cars: https://www.ft.com/content/7980e98e-d8b6-11e8-a854-33d6f82e62f8
6. Google, Adding Sound Effect Information to YouTube Captions: https://ai.googleblog.com/2017/03/adding-sound-effect-information-to.html
7. Nature, Clinically applicable deep learning for diagnosis and referral in retinal disease: https://www.nature.com/articles/s41591-018-0107-6
8. Google, Using large-scale brain simulations for machine learning and A.I.: https://googleblog.blogspot.com/2012/06/using-large-scale-brain-simulations-for.html
9. Wired, Google's AI Wins First Historic Match: https://www.wired.com/2016/03/googles-ai-wins-first-game-historic-match-go-champion/

3
AMAZON

Using Deep Learning To Drive Business Performance

Jeff Bezos founded Amazon as an online book store, but in reality he could have sold anything. His main focus was establishing a technology company that could dominate during the predicted boom in online retail, which he saw coming. Today, Amazon is a multinational e-commerce giant and the world's leading cloud computing provider, making it the third most valuable public company in the United States. Beyond its core retail and cloud business, the company also has a publishing business, a film and television studio operation, and produces consumer products such as the Kindle e-readers, Fire tablets and TV sticks, as well as the Amazon Echo.

Amazon has used predictive analytics since those earliest days in the 1990s. It has experience deploying these systems across its entire business – from its famous recommendation engines to optimizing the routes of robots working in its order fulfilment centers.

However, the growing power of machine learning has caused the online retail giant to reassess every aspect of its operations since the start of the current decade. Not content with merely competing with Walmart and Target for the retail market, it has always positioned itself as a rival to Google, Facebook and Apple, seeking leadership in the tech sphere.

This meant implementing deep learning technology into its core services, as well as expanding into new areas such as home automation with its Alexa-powered Echo devices and cashier-free retail stores.

Looking ahead, Amazon has grand plans involving automated delivery drones and "anticipatory shipping", which will attempt to read your mind and ship products to you before you even order them!

How Does Amazon Use Artificial Intelligence?

Amazon pioneered the recommendation engine – search engines designed to sell us things – which has been the core of its business strategy since the beginning. Over the years, the analytics behind the scenes have become more sophisticated but it has always worked by segmenting customers according to the data it collects about them, modelling their behavior and matching them with items popular with others who fit a similar pattern.

In early 2014, the company began the single biggest overhaul of its recommendation system to date, when it started to implement deep learning algorithms into its prediction tools.[1] Deep learning is now built into many of the site's features, which are designed to present the user with a more personalized shopping experience, such as its "frequently bought together" and "customers who bought this also bought …" recommendations.

Deep learning uses deeply layered neural networks that mimic human brains in the way they "learn" from the data that passes through them. These algorithms are capable of adapting themselves to become increasingly efficient at spotting patterns and relationships in data, in this case Amazon's transactional and customer behavioral data. They now power Amazon's recommendation engine just as they do Google's searches, Facebook's feeds and Netflix's movie suggestions. Like its rivals for the tech crown, Amazon is confidently backing deep learning as the technology that will power the artificial intelligence (AI) revolution.

Another key use case at Amazon is found in its fulfilment centers – warehouses where the millions of customer orders placed every day are picked and packed by humans working alongside sophisticated, AI-powered robots. When observed as a static, stand-alone piece of machinery, Amazon's warehouse robots may not look like much – simply squat, mobile platforms.[2] But driven by deep learning algorithms, they are able to efficiently route their way around labyrinthine stacks of portable shelves, locate whatever items are required and move them to the human picker who completes the assembly of each order. As robots can operate in far tighter conditions than humans, this initiative helps Amazon maximize the space available for stock in its warehouses, increasing revenue as orders can be filled more quickly. One hundred thousand of these robots are currently deployed in Amazon fulfilment centers around the world.[3]

Amazon Alexa

It's strange to think that the AI-powered personal home assistant device almost seemed like a novelty when Amazon first introduced it in 2015. As of 2018 they are a feature in 16% of US homes, and that figure looks set to increase as Amazon, along with Google, continue to improve, refine and market their devices.[4]

Amazon's breakthrough was to realize that the biggest factor limiting uptake of AI in the home wasn't the technology itself, which had matured to the point where it is more than capable of assisting with basic domestic tasks. It was the interface itself – while smartphones have become increasingly useful, they often still aren't as simple to use as, say, a light switch, kettle, radio or recipe book.

Echo made it straightforward for us to communicate using our voices with smart home devices, as well as a handy portal for quick information, or playing background music while we go about house-hold chores.

The accuracy with which it can interpret our voice commands is due to Amazon's implementation of deep learning within its natural language algorithms.[5] Neural networks are used to detect the user's "wake word", which tells the device to start listening for and interpret-ing a command. As it processes voice commands it becomes increas-ingly efficient at understanding the nuanced ways human beings use spoken language. Effectively, the deep neural network "learns" about how we talk from the voice data it processes.

Amazon's Artificial Intelligence Flywheel

Amazon's model for propagating the use of AI across its variety of business operations has been referred to as a "flywheel".[6] The name is taken from a class of mechanical devices designed to efficiently store energy generated by a power source and moderate its rate of release. The idea is that excess "energy" generated by successful deployments of AI in one part of the business will fuel research and investment in another part.

This approach helped to foster an environment where data and tech-nology are shared between departments and business units, which are able to learn from best practice guidelines established by oth-ers. For example, the improvements in recommendation engine accu-racy brought about by the deployment of deep learning became a key driver behind its adoption by the team working on Echo's voice capabilities.

In turn, other units at Amazon realized they could capitalize on the widespread adoption of Alexa-equipped devices into homes – par-ticularly the ability to create custom applications known as "skills", which can be invoked through the device. This led to skills being added to let users access services such as Amazon Prime Video and

Amazon Music Unlimited with their voices. And, in turn, deep learning has also been integrated into the way Alexa decides which of its 40,000 skills a user will find most useful, based on the words they speak.[7]

Amazon realized that successful deep learning initiatives pay for themselves, not just by enabling the business processes that they are deployed in to operate more efficiently, but also by generating more data with which to train algorithms deployed in different processes.

Amazon Web Services

Just like its competitors Google and Alibaba, Amazon sells cloud-based computing services to its business customers under its Amazon Web Services (AWS) brand. In recent years it has built machine learning services into this offering, meaning businesses can "hire" AI capabilities at a fraction of the cost of building their own infrastructure.

With the race to adopt AI among businesses in all sectors, providing tools to help smaller businesses compete has become a core business strategy for Amazon. After all, as the old adage goes, those most likely to get rich out of a gold rush are those who are selling the shovels!

AWS provides access to core machine learning technologies, such as natural language processing and computer vision, as well as tools that can put them to use extracting actionable insights from unstructured voice or video data.[8]

Amazon Prime Air

One of Amazon's more ambitious projects involves rolling out fleets of airborne drones to deliver packages directly to our homes. When it was announced in 2013, its mission was to enable Amazon to make deliveries within 30 minutes of a customer placing an order.[9]

Since then Amazon has carried out the first trial deliveries by drones from its fulfilment center in Cambridge, England.

Machine learning is a fundamental part of the systems that control the drones.[10] Although it has been going for several years, the project is still a long way from general use and there are regulatory hurdles to be overcome. Amazon has not publicly spoken in detail about the technology of the drones, but it is likely that they employ computer vision to help them navigate around obstacles and identify safe landing spots.

Key Challenges, Learning Points And Takeaways

- Amazon was one of the first online businesses to harness the power of predictive analytics. AI – which promises more accurate predictions than any technology so far – is a natural next step for it.

- Amazon has built a corporate strategy that it calls a "flywheel" to encourage distribution of energy, momentum and data generated by AI initiatives throughout its network of business operations.

- Advances won through building deep learning capabilities into its recommendation engine algorithms inspired further use of the technology, feeding into development of its Alexa voice assistant and its Amazon Prime Air drone delivery service.

- Amazon is enabling other businesses to automate and take advantage of AI. It does this by leasing its machine learning and deep learning technology as a service through its AWS platform.

Notes

1. Wired, Inside Amazon's Artificial Intelligence Flywheel: https://www.wired.com/story/amazon-artificial-intelligence-flywheel/
2. Robots, Drive Unit: https://robots.ieee.org/robots/kiva/?utm_source=spectrum
3. IEEE Spectrum, Brad Porter, VP of Robotics at Amazon, on Warehouse Automation, Machine Learning, and His First Robot: https://spectrum.ieee.org/automaton/robotics/industrial-robots/interview-brad-porter-vp-of-robotics-at-amazon
4. Tech Crunch, 39 million Americans now own a smart speaker, report claims: https://techcrunch.com/2018/01/12/39-million-americans-now-own-a-smart-speaker-report-claims/
5. Quora, How does Amazon use Deep Learning?: https://www.quora.com/How-does-Amazon-use-Deep-Learning
6. Wired, Inside Amazon's Artificial Intelligence Flywheel: https://www.wired.com/story/amazon-artificial-intelligence-flywheel/
7. Amazon, The Scalable Neural Architecture behind Alexa's Ability to Select Skills: https://developer.amazon.com/blogs/alexa/post/4e6db03f-6048-4b62-ba4b-6544da9ac440/the-scalable-neural-architecture-behind-alexa-s-ability-to-arbitrate-skills
8. Amazon, Machine Learning on AWS: https://aws.amazon.com/machine-learning/
9. CBS, Amazon unveils futuristic plan: delivery by drone: https://www.cbsnews.com/news/amazon-unveils-futuristic-plan-delivery-by-drone/
10. Amazon, Machine Learning on AWS: https://aws.amazon.com/machine-learning/

4
APPLE

Integrating AI Into Products And Protecting User Privacy

Apple is the world's largest information technology company by revenue. The California-based company designs, develops and sells iconic smart tech products such as the iPhone, iPad, Macs, Apple Watch, Apple TV, as well as accompanying software and services. In 2018, Apple became the first-ever public company to be valued at over US$1 trillion.[1]

Apple's artificial intelligence (AI) strategy centers around its devices, and in recent years the company has positioned itself as a pioneer of in-device AI technology, citing its superior security and potential for creating unique, user-engaging experiences.

How Does Apple Use Artificial Intelligence?

Apple's vision for the future is powerful handheld devices that are capable of running their own machine learning on datasets gathered via their own array of sensors. This is clearly at odds with the vision of a future dominated by cloud computing and relatively low-powered terminals often championed by other tech companies.

This means running machine learning algorithms directly on their devices using powerful central processing unit or graphics processing unit chips built into their phones, watches or speakers.

One current example is the development of the Neural Engine inside the latest iPhone X models.[2] This is a custom-designed chip specifically designed for carrying out the neural net calculations needed for deep learning. This makes it faster to process functions such as Face ID logins, features in the camera that help users take better pictures (or add silly effects), augmented reality and managing battery life.[3]

Running machine learning on devices can also be far faster than having to wait until data is returned from the cloud before insights can become actionable. However, it isn't without disadvantages. Only being trainable on data gathered from one device means those algorithms won't have the benefit of learning from the huge, crowdsourced datasets that cloud machine learning can plug into.

This ties in with Apple's focus on safeguarding users' data. By ensuring that sensitive personal data doesn't have to leave the phone before it can be processed by machine learning, it hopes consumers will trust their data is safer with them.

Apple's proprietary AI ecosphere centers around its Core ML framework. Core ML allows developers to build machine learning algorithms into products, including deep learning, computer vision and natural language. It powers the smarts behind Siri, Apple's voice assistant, as well as the AI functionality in iPhone cameras and QuickType keyboards.[4]

Smarter Apps

A significant part of the credit for the iPhone's success has to go to the App Store. Smartphone users had been downloading apps to their phones for a while when it was launched in 2008, but Apple's streamlined store meant iPhone users could customize and add features to their phones more intuitively than was previously possible.

Cognisant of the way its app ecosystem keeps customers coming back to Apple year after year when their mobile contracts are up for renewal, it has pushed developers to integrate AI into their third-party apps. This tactic is aimed at continuing to provide compelling functionality that isn't available on other mobile platforms. To this end, Apple has provided developers with tools such as Create ML, which enable them to power apps with machine learning running on users' devices.

A great example is an app called Homecourt, which was designed to assist with refereeing amateur basketball games. All a user needs to do is point the camera at a game in play, and the machine learning will tag the players in the game, logging when they pass and shoot, as well as recording their position on the court. All this is done through computer vision technology running on the device itself.[5]

Another app, known as Polyword, allows users to get the name of whatever object they are pointing their camera at in any one of 30 languages, using computer vision and machine learning.[6]

Other features allow it to take a critical look at the photographs you are shooting and suggest improvements in real time, and manage notifications to make it more likely important information is brought to your attention at the right time.

Natural Language Processing

When Apple launched Siri it became the first widely used AI-enabled and natural language processing (NLP)-powered assistant. Although it has been criticized for a lack of innovation compared to that seen in competitor AIs,[7] recent updates brought in real-time, machine learning-driven translation between 40 pairs of languages.

Siri's NLP functions do send information into the cloud. However, user privacy is preserved by the fact that all identifying information is stripped from the voice command data before it leaves the user's device in an encrypted form.

Recent NLP research at Apple has focused on giving Siri users more accurate results when they search for information on businesses or points of interest in their local area.[8] Researchers introduced location signals into the training data, giving Siri access to localized datasets, including place names and small businesses. In theory it will use the location data while it interprets spoken language to add to its understanding of what the user might mean. Alexa will have a better chance at guessing, for example, if someone who utters the words "I'm going to Kilkenny" intends to visit the town in Ireland or murder a man called Kenny.

Key Challenges, Learning Points And Takeaways

- AI is very much at the heart of Apple's strategy, which is to build it into the fabric of its devices and supporting services.

- Apple is prioritizing user privacy over an ability to pump all data into the cloud to train algorithms on bigger data sets.

- It is also promoting the use of its proprietary machine learning platform Create ML to make apps that will only work on its devices, creating exclusivity within its own app ecosphere.

Notes

1. https://www.theguardian.com/technology/2018/aug/02/apple-becomes-worlds-first-trillion-dollar-company
2. Wired, Apple's Neural Engine Infuses the IPhone with AI Smarts: https://www.wired.com/story/apples-neural-engine-infuses-the-iphone-with-ai-smarts/

3. CNBC, https://www.cnbc.com/2018/09/12/apple-upgrades-neural-engine-in-iphone-xsa12-bionic-chip.html
4. Apple, Get Ready for Core ML 2: https://developer.apple.com/machine-learning/
5. Wired, Apple's Plan to Bring Artificial Intelligence to Your Home: https://www.wired.com/story/apples-plans-to-bring-artificial-intelligence-to-your-phone/
6. Github, Polyword: https://github.com/Binb1/Polyword
7. Wall Street Journal, "I'm Not Sure I Understand" – How Apple's Siri Lost Her Mojo: https://www.wsj.com/articles/apples-siri-once-an-original-now-struggles-to-be-heard-above-the-crowd-1496849095
8. Apple, Finding Local Destinations with Siri's Regionally Specific Language Models for Speech Recognition: https://machinelearning.apple.com/2018/08/09/regionally-specific-language-models.html

5
BAIDU

Machine Learning For Search Engines And Autonomous Cars

Baidu is a Chinese technology company that focuses on internet-related services and products. The company operates the most popular search engine in China, giving it access to the vast datasets generated by billions of search queries. On top of that, Baidu is also an app developer, runs an advertisement platform and is recognized and supported by the Chinese government for its work around developing self-driving vehicles. Its Project Apollo is one of the most mature autonomous driving programs in the world. In 2018, Baidu became the first Chinese artificial intelligence (AI) company to join the Partnership on AI established by Facebook, Amazon, Google, Microsoft and IBM to encourage ethical development of AI.[1]

How Does Baidu Use Artificial Intelligence?

As well as a search function, Baidu also offers image searching, maps, videos, news and translation services to its users. AI has been deployed across all of these functions to more accurately return results that users will find useful.

This is helped by the fact there are more than 800 million internet users in China – more than twice the total population of the United States,[2] which means that AI algorithms have a far bigger pool of data to work with.

Baidu collectively labels all of its AI operations as Baidu Brain. The platform, currently on version 3, offers access to 110 AI technologies, including natural language processing, image recognition, facial recognition and automated labelling of video data. It also includes the EasyDL tool, which allows development of deep learning systems without the need for any coding.

At a conference hosted by Baidu in Beijing in July 2018, a doctor with no programming skills used the platform and was able to develop a deep learning tool capable of identifying 40 types of parasitic worm, which is now being clinically tested.[3]

Self-Driving Cars

Baidu was chosen above its Chinese rivals as the nation's "champion" for the development of fully autonomous vehicles. The company is aiming to have self-driving cars on the roads of Beijing by 2019,[4] and begin mass production by 2021.[5]

To get there, it launched Project Apollo, which involves partnerships with several high-profile car makers, including Ford and Hyundai.[6]

AI is crucial to autonomous driving. The cars are equipped with sensors connected to machine learning algorithms in the cloud and running locally in the vehicle to enable them to "see" conditions and hazards on the road.

Baidu's cars also use high-resolution 3D mapping data, collected from satellite imagery as well as by camera-equipped cars that have built detailed image databases covering China's road system.[7]

Ford's cars will take part in the first tests scheduled for early next year, when they will be fitted with Baidu's Virtual Driver System. This system is capable of giving the cars "level 4" autonomous driving ability, based on the Society of Auto Engineers (SAE) level system.

The SAE has defined five levels of autonomy, ranging from level 0 (no automation) to level 5, which is "full automation" – meaning the car can drive itself anywhere a human would be capable of driving it. Level 4 – which Baidu intends to road test next year – requires a car to be able to carry out all of the driver functions, with no need for the human driver to pay attention.[8]

As well as cars, the open source Apollo Virtual Driver System can be fitted to trucks, giving them the ability to operate autonomously within geofenced areas of open highway.

Mobile Artificial Intelligence

Baidu has partnered with Huawei to build an open AI platform for mobile development. The aim is to provide mobile users with "AI that knows you better", making it more convenient than ever to use the functions and services we're used to accessing through our phones.[9]

It will let developers write code that will run machine learning tasks on the neural processing unit circuitry built into Huawei's phones. They will be able to take advantage of the voice and image recognition abilities of machine learning, as well as its suitability for building augmented reality apps. The move puts it into competition with Apple and Samsung, which are both developing their own mobile AI frameworks internally.

Real-Time Translation

Baidu has also developed a handheld device capable of generating deep learning translations between English, Mandarin Chinese and

Japanese.[10] It is currently aimed at the tourist market, assisting users to navigate their way around foreign cities and carry out tasks such as ordering food in restaurants and using public transport. It uses deep learning natural language processing algorithms, and translation is carried out in the cloud.[11]

Key Challenges, Learning Points And Takeaways

- The huge population of its native country – around half of whom are online – has helped Baidu collect a vast dataset of consumer profiles and behaviors. This is used to streamline services, as well as sell to advertisers to allow them to more accurately target their campaigns.

- Baidu offers AI services to businesses to enable them to develop and release their own AI-powered applications under its Baidu Brain framework.

- Although Baidu was slow to catch on to mobile, it is making up for lost ground now through a strategic partnership with China's largest smartphone manufacturer, Huawei, to put AI inside phones.

- Baidu has China's, and possibly the world's, most advanced autonomous vehicle program, with cars powered by its Apollo technology expected to bring level 4 autonomy to the roads soon.

Notes

1. CNN, Silicon Valley is working with China to ease fears about AI: https://amp.cnn.com/cnn/2018/10/17/tech/baidu-artificial-intelligence -china/index.html
2. Forbes, China Now Boasts More Than 800 Million Internet Users And 98% Of Them Are Mobile: https://www.forbes.com/sites/

niallmccarthy/2018/08/23/china-now-boasts-more-than-800-million-internet-users-and-98-of-them-are-mobile-infographic/#21c9e8807092

3. Tech Republic, Baidu no-code EasyDL tool could democratize AI for small businesses, bridge talent gap: https://www.techrepublic.com/article/baidu-no-code-easydl-tool-could-democratize-ai-for-small-businesses-bridge-talent-gap/#ftag=RSS56d97e7

4. Reuters, https://www.reuters.com/article/autos-selfdriving-baidu/chinas-baidu-gets-green-light-for-self-driving-vehicle-tests-in-beijing-idUSL3N1R51A5

5. Tech Crunch, Baidu plans to mass produce Level 4 self-driving cars with BAIC by 2021: https://techcrunch.com/2017/10/13/baidu-plans-to-mass-produce-level-4-self-driving-cars-with-baic-by-2021/

6. Ford, Ford and Baidu Announce Joint Autonomous Vehicle Testing: https://media.ford.com/content/fordmedia/fna/us/en/news/2018/10/31/ford-and-baidu-announce-joint-autonomous-vehicle-testing.html

7. Bloomberg, Wanted in China: Detailed Maps for 30 Million Self-Driving Cars: https://www.bloomberg.com/news/articles/2018-08-22/wanted-in-china-detailed-maps-for-30-million-self-driving-cars

8. SAE, Taxonomy and Definitions for Terms Related to Driving Automation Systems for On-Road Motor Vehicles: https://www.sae.org/standards/content/j3016_201806/

9. Huawei, Huawei and Baidu Sign Strategic Agreement to Lead the New Era of Mobile AI: https://www.huawei.com/en/press-events/news/2017/12/huawei-baidu-strategic-agreement-mobileai

10. Digital Trends: https://www.digitaltrends.com/cool tech/baidu machine-translator/

11. MIT Technology Review, Baidu Shows Off Its Instant Pocket Translator: https://www.technologyreview.com/s/610623/baidu-shows-off-its-instant-pocket-translator/

6
FACEBOOK

Using Artificial Intelligence To Improve Social Media Services

Facebook is a US-based, multinational social media and social networking company. It has been a part of the fabric of modern-day life for over a decade now. Around 2.2 billion[1] people use the Facebook social media platform to keep up to date with friends and family, arrange their social lives, find local businesses and, of course, share pictures of their pets with the world.

Every time any one of us uses Facebook we generate data – what we are doing, where we are, who we are with. Before social media, we didn't have anywhere to upload the 136,000 images per minute we currently add to Facebook, let alone the 510,000 comments and 293,000 status updates.[2]

All that data is great training fodder for artificial intelligence (AI), too – and the company has launched a number of tools and projects that put machine learning in the service of its users.

How Does Facebook Use Artificial Intelligence?

Facebook uses its AI engine, FBLearner Flow, to personalize users' news feeds and homepages, putting information (and advertising) in front of them, which it believes they will find useful or of interest.[3]

It uses machine learning to analyze and segment the platform's billions of users, generally according to information the users provide themselves – where they live, work, who they are friends with, where they travel to, what they search for online and what their signals (such as "likes" and "shares") suggest about them.

Monitoring Content

As well as filling news feeds with interesting updates and stories, the machine learning algorithms also work to filter out content such as violence or nudity, which it doesn't allow users to post on the service.

One focus in this area has been a crackdown on distributors of "fake news" – either politically motivated or when done by fraudsters hoping to make money. Machine learning algorithms are used in conjunction with manual and automated fact-checking services.[4] When stories are flagged, either by machines or humans, as fake, their spread across Facebook's network can be tracked, and steps taken to prevent users from being harmed. This could include deleting the material or flagging it as likely to be false.

Facial Recognition

One area of AI research where Facebook is head and shoulders above the competition is facial recognition technology, which is hardly surprising, considering how many pictures of people's faces it has on its servers.

The technology is called Deep Face, and it's what springs into action when you upload a photograph and Facebook starts to suggest who it thinks is in the picture. It uses neural networks to parse 68 data points from every face it analyzes, measuring facial features, colouring and proportion.

It was fed over 4 million facial images to train it how to recognize individual facial elements, and understand how facial characteristics give each human a unique look. When another facial image it analyzes matches or closely fits a unique pattern it has already recorded, then it knows there is a higher probability that it has two pictures of the same person.

As well as conveniently tagging people in your photographs, Facebook has also used the technology to help users to keep track of where photos of themselves are cropping up on the site, and also to create audio descriptions of photographs to help the visually impaired.[5]

Facebook says that its facial recognition algorithms have a success rate of 97.35% when used with publicly available test datasets – very close to human-level accuracy.[6]

Understanding Text

AI is also used by Facebook to wring insights from the half a million text comments posted to the site every minute. Its aim here is to use contextual analysis to get a deeper understanding of what we're trying to say, and offer information or services that we might find useful without us having to ask for them. An example that Facebook gives is that machine learning algorithms "listening in" on a conversation between friends about a journey they have to make might automatically throw up links to ride-hailing services operating in the locality.[7]

A more advanced implementation being explored would step in when a user makes a post saying they have, for example, a bicycle that they want to sell. It might automatically generate an advert-style post, discern the correct selling price based on the user's description and direct them to local selling pages where they may find a buyer.

This system is called Deep Text, because it relies on deep learning neural networks to analyze text and understand not just the words, but how the meaning of a word depends on its placement within a post and the other words used with it. This is a form of semi-unsupervised learning because rather than relying on a set of rules, such as a dictionary or a grammar rulebook, it learns for itself how words are used by "listening" to them – much the same way as a human does.

Suicide Prevention

Facebook also uses AI to monitor the way its users engage with the service, and looks for signs that individuals may be depressed or in danger of hurting themselves.[8]

It does this by looking for patterns in a user's posting behavior that match those of other posts that have previously been flagged as containing indicators that someone may be suicidal.

Signs could include users directly talking about themselves suffering or being unhappy, or receiving lots of messages from friends expressing concern or asking if they need help.

Once an alarm is raised, it is reviewed by human specialists before a decision is made on whether to intervene by offering the user information on how to receive help.

The social network doesn't currently contact users directly, preferring to put information at their fingertips in a timely way. But it has examined the possibility of alerting a user's real-world "support network" of friends and family. However, that would clearly have significant privacy implications.

FBLearner Flow

The "backbone" of Facebook's AI technology is its FBLearner Flow platform. It is designed to allow computer engineers to deploy AI in any area of the company's operation, without the engineer having to be a machine learning specialist.[9]

It is now in use by over 25% of Facebook's engineering teams, and is responsible for making 6 million predictions per second for the business and its customers. It is designed to be used to create algorithms that can easily be reused among multiple Facebook projects, once they have proven themselves effective.

Facebook AI Research

Facebook's machine learning research and development is coordinated through its Facebook AI Research division. Areas of research include ways in which smart, learning computer technology can be integrated with Facebook's services, how improvements can be made to core AI disciplines such as natural language processing and computer vision, and even how the future of socializing is likely to be shaped by augmented and virtual reality technology.

This year Facebook announced plans to grow the division to around 170 data scientists and engineers spread across its global offices, which include sites in Montreal, Pittsburgh, Paris, London and Tel Aviv.[10]

Key Challenges, Learning Points And Takeaways

- The vast amount of information we share about our lives on Facebook means that the company has access to more of our personal data than just about anyone else.

- Facebook has leveraged this to build features that keep us coming back to the site (and sharing more data), as well as match us with advertisers whose products we might want to buy.

- All of this data – including our photos and text – has been invaluable to Facebook when it comes to training its facial recognition and natural language processing algorithms.

- Unprecedented levels of insight into our lives means it can make increasingly accurate predictions about us – from what we want to buy to whether we are thinking about killing ourselves.

Notes

1. Statistica, Number of monthly active Facebook users worldwide as of 2nd quarter 2018 (in millions): https://www.statista.com/statistics/264810/number-of-monthly-active-facebook-users-worldwide/
2. Zephoria, Top 15 Valuable Facebook Statistics: https://zephoria.com/top-15-valuable-facebook-statistics/
3. Facebook, Introducing FBLearner Flow: Facebook's AI backbone: https://code.fb.com/core-data/introducing-fblearner-flow-facebook-s-ai-backbone/
4. Facebook, Increasing Our Efforts to Fight False News: https://newsroom.fb.com/news/2018/06/increasing-our-efforts-to-fight-false-news/
5. Facebook, Managing Your Identity on Facebook with Face Recognition Technology: https://newsroom.fb.com/news/2017/12/managing-your-identity-on-facebook-with-face-recognition-technology/
6. Facebook, DeepFace: Closing the Gap to Human-Level Performance in Face Verification: https://research.fb.com/publications/deepface-closing-the-gap-to-human-level-performance-in-face-verification/
7. Facebook, Introducing DeepText: Facebook's text understanding engine: https://code.fb.com/core-data/introducing-deeptext-facebook-s-text-understanding-engine/
8. BBC, Facebook artificial intelligence spots suicidal users: https://www.bbc.co.uk/news/technology-39126027
9. Facebook, Introducing FBLearner Flow: Facebook's AI backbone: https://code.fb.com/core-data/introducing-fblearner-flow-facebook-s-ai-backbone/
10. Washington Post, Facebook, boosting artificial-intelligence research, says it's "not going fast enough": https://www.washingtonpost.com/technology/2018/07/17/facebook-boosting-artificial-intelligence-research-says-its-not-going-fast-enough/?utm_term=.de4f2c7f1298

7
IBM

Cognitive Computing Helps Machines
Debate With Humans

IBM is the granddaddy of the computer industry, having been in existence for over 100 years. Constantly innovating, it dominated the mainframe industry in the 1960s and 1970s before pioneering the personal computer concept in the 1980s.

Like other US tech giants, it was not slow to understand the importance of machine learning. Its best known artificial intelligence (AI) endeavor is IBM Watson, a "cognitive computing" platform that became famous when it defeated two long-standing human champions at the gameshow *Jeopardy!*[1]

Since then Watson has been deployed across thousands of business use cases, and continues to be used by IBM to demonstrate the power and flexibility of its machine learning technology.

How Does IBM Use Artificial Intelligence?

As well as winning television gameshows, Watson has been deployed in many industries where its natural language processing capabilities are driving efficiency and creating new opportunities.

It was originally envisaged as a question-and-answer engine, but over the years its applications have diversified as its skillset has grown.

Royal Bank of Scotland uses Watson to power its customer service chatbot, Cora. Cora was trained on over 1,000 responses to 200 customer service queries. It then continues to learn after it is deployed, building links between natural language questions posed by human customers and the responses it has stored in its database.[2] If a conversation becomes too difficult it will pass the customer to a human agent.

The rate at which Cora manages to handle queries by itself without having to resort to human assistance is known as the "containment rate" and is a key metric of its success. Currently, the rate is around 40% (and up to 80% for queries around commercial banking issues).[3] The idea is that this rate will start to increase as the bot gains more experience of interacting with humans.

Stationery giant Staples used Watson to build a "smart ordering" system called the Easy Button. Essentially a voice-activated assistant similar to Amazon's Alexa, it is specifically trained in anticipating the stationery needs of Staples' business customers. As it is repeatedly used it comes to learn about brands and quantities that customers require.[4]

Watson has broken into sports too. The All England Lawn Tennis Club worked with IBM at the world-famous Wimbledon tournaments to deliver automated highlights and enhance fan engagement. Trained with data from 22 years of tennis covering over 53 million data points, Watson was taught to deliver automated commentary, as well as real-time stats and analytics, directly to fans. A Watson-powered app called Ask Fred (named after Fred Perry) was also created to answer fans' questions, from the history of tennis to where they can find public toilets at Wimbledon.[5]

Watson is also widely used in healthcare. The American Cancer Society used Watson to create the first AI assistant aimed at helping people diagnosed with cancer, and Watson For Oncology is a clinical support platform that advises doctors on treatment decisions, using thousands of pages of medical documents and case notes to predict treatment paths that are likely to have the best outcomes.[6]

If there was one task that common sense would seem to dictate that AI cannot yet do, it would be designing perfume. Global fragrance giant Symrise, which makes scents for Estee Lauder, Avon and Donna Karan, among others, thought differently. The result of their work with IBM is called Phylira, and it has developed scents – usually the preserve of human experts who have trained for years – that will soon be on sale in 4,000 Brazilian beauty stores.

Phylira works by breaking down scents into their constituent parts – the different oils, chemicals and natural extracts that are used to add specific flavors to each perfume, 1.7 million of them all together. It then read in sales data and customer service data to draw links showing which combinations of scents were likely to be appealing to different demographic groups.

The two fragrances that were developed by the algorithm achieved "stellar" results in focus group testing, proving more popular than other scents that had previously sold successfully to the target demographic (Brazilian millennials).[7]

Watson has certainly grown into a phenomenal success story for IBM since it stole the *Jeopardy!* crown. Aside from these use cases, Watson is also used by seven of the world's top 10 automotive companies and eight of the top 10 largest oil and gas companies.[8]

Project Debater

Perhaps the most impressive application of IBM's language processing AI technology is found in its Project Debater.

IBM says that Project Debater is the first AI system that can debate humans on complex subjects. It uses language processing and a database of hundreds of millions of articles covering 100 subject areas.[9]

It uses these tools and data to listen to its opponent's point of view, considers it, and then challenges it on logical and ethical grounds.

In its first live, public debate, Project Debater took on two experienced college debaters on the topics of whether space exploration should be government subsidized, and whether more telemedicine (medical practice carried out remotely by a doctor) would be a good thing.

On the subject of telemedicine, the audience voted that IBM's AI put forward a more compelling argument than its human opponent.[10]

Although overall the event was considered a draw, it marks a meaningful step forward for AI language processing. The technology has progressed from recognizing individual words, as has been done by email spam filtering for decades, to being able to answer basic questions (as seen in Siri and Alexa), to being able to engage in open, free-form debate.

Rather than analyzing a human sentence semantically, and trying to figure out what it wants to know, it must be able to discern a point that is being made, then construct an argument against it. It can do this either by citing authoritative facts that suggest the original point is based on bad information, or by finding logical flaws in the statements being made.

This technique of language processing is known as argument mining. In IBM's use case, it further broke this down into argument detection and argument stance classification. The former analyzes the argument to determine the claims that are being made and the evidence they are based on. The latter determines where those argument components sit in relation to the polarity of the discussion.[11]

It's worth noting that although Project Debater appears to be able to tackle any subject, it's still an example of specialized AI, rather than the fully generalized AI, which is still not likely to be around for some time. Although it has expert level knowledge on many subjects, it is only trained to apply that knowledge to debate. It would require further training for it to be able to use it for other purposes, for example, education.

While it mainly serves as an impressive display of AI competency right now, in the future IBM theorizes that the rules it is built on (and those it develops itself) will help humans choose decision outcomes that are evidence based, rather than influenced by bias, faulty logic or ambiguity.

Key Challenges, Learning Points And Takeaways

- Thousands of businesses are using IBM Watson to take advantage of AI. Particularly active areas of work include customer relations, chatbots and medicine.

- By focusing on language processing capabilities, IBM's strategy is to break down communication barriers between people and machines, making it easier for us to harness their potential.

- IBM uses gameplay to demonstrate that its cognitive systems are capable of learning to solve puzzles in the same way that humans do, and with practice can become better than them. This began with Deep Blue's defeat of Kasparov and continues with Project Debater.

- Project Debater represents AI evolving past its current ability to answer questions, and towards being able to engage in natural human conversations. This could have all sorts of implications for the future of AI.

Notes

1. Tech Republic, IBM Watson: The inside story of how the Jeopardy-winning supercomputer was born, and what it wants to do next: https://www.techrepublic.com/article/ibm-watson-the-inside-story-of-how-the-jeopardy-winning-supercomputer-was-born-and-what-it-wants-to-do-next/
2. IBM, Raising Cora: https://www.ibm.com/industries/banking-financial-markets/front-office/chatbots-banking
3. IBM, Putting Smart to Work: https://www.ibm.com/blogs/insights-on-business/banking/putting-smart-work-raising-cora/
4. IBM, How Staples is making customer service "easy" with Watson Conversation: https://www.ibm.com/blogs/watson/2017/02/staples-making-customer-service-easy-watson-conversation/
5. IBM, How Wimbledon is using IBM Watson AI to power highlights, analytics and enriched fan experiences: https://www.ibm.com/blogs/watson/2017/07/ibm-watsons-ai-is-powering-wimbledon-highlights-analytics-and-a-fan-experiences/
6. American Cancer Society, American Cancer Society and IBM Collaborate to Create Virtual Cancer Health Advisor: http://pressroom.cancer.org/WatsonACSLaunch
7. Vox, Is AI the future of perfume? IBM is betting on it: https://www.vox.com/the-goods/2018/10/24/18019918/ibm-artificial-intelligence-perfume-symrise-philyra
8. IBM, IBM Largest Ever AI Toolset Release Is Tailor Made for 9 Industries and Professions: https://newsroom.ibm.com/2018-09-24-IBM-Largest-Ever-AI-Toolset-Release-Is-Tailor-Made-for-9-Industries-and-Professions
9. The Verge, What it's like to watch an IBM AI successfully debate humans: https://www.theverge.com/2018/6/18/17477686/ibm-project-debater-ai
10. The Guardian, Man 1, machine 1: landmark debate between AI and humans ends in draw: https://www.theguardian.com/technology/2018/jun/18/artificial-intelligence-ibm-debate-project-debater
11. IBM, Project Debater Datasets: https://www.research.ibm.com/haifa/dept/vst/debating_data.shtml

8
JD.COM

Automating Retail With Artificial Intelligence

JD.com is one of the largest online retailers in China and a company that prides itself on high tech and artificial intelligence (AI) enabled processes, which include a drone delivery system, autonomous delivery vehicles and robot-automated fulfilment centers.

We talked to a lot of businesses when putting this book together and although they all have different ideas about the future of AI, there is one thing most of them are at pains to agree on: AI isn't here to threaten human jobs and make us redundant, but to augment our own abilities.

JD.com's founder Liu Qiangdong (also known as Richard Liu) is the exception. In a World Retail Congress 2018 interview he said: "I hope my company would be a 100% automation company. I hope that someday there will be no human beings any more. 100% operated by the AI and the robots."[1]

You might suspect he is simply being more honest than most tech CEOs, who in reality would love to be able to do away with soft, squishy and demanding humans entirely (in their businesses, at least).

However, it gives a telling insight into JD.com's strategy for rolling out AI, which has focused on using robotics to physically automate as much of its retail operations as possible.

What Does JD.com Use Artificial Intelligence For?

JD.com's big push into AI has focused on deploying it to handle delivery, logistics and supply chain tasks across its vast retail network.

In fact, at its flagship Shanghai fulfilment center, which processes 200,000 orders per day, it employs a total of four people.[2]

Robots, powered by machine learning, move crates of products onto snaking networks of conveyor belts, which distribute items that are ready to be packed to other robots, which box them up and despatch them for delivery.

The extent to which AI has been built into JD.com's logistics is what has made it possible for them to offer a next-day delivery service to virtually any of China's 1.3 billion residents, no matter where in the country's 10 million km^2 of territory they live. Now they are making preparations for the jump to same-day delivery.[3]

Of course, it is also using AI to improve customer experience. The company has even produced a chatbot that is capable of producing an automated piece of poetry, to be supplied to the recipient when items are purchased as gifts. The buyer can input characteristics of the person who will receive the gift and details of the occasion, and the robot will do the rest – how romantic!

The company has also partnered with China's social media giants, Tencent and Baidu, to integrate its products into their hugely popular messaging and image-sharing apps. Once again AI plays a key part in this. It is used to match users, based on their profile data, with items sold by JD.com that might appeal to them. These appear as sponsored advertisements, and users can order and pay for them without leaving their social apps.[4]

Automated Deliveries By Air And Road

In 2016, while Amazon was carrying out its first test deliveries using unmanned aerial vehicles, JD.com was putting its drone delivery network into full operation. Drone delivery has been a reality in China ever since, with JD.com's fleet having completed over 300,000 minutes of flight time so far.[5]

JD.com is working on drones that can deliver cargo weighing up to 5 tons. Currently, the drone service is mainly used to deliver to areas that are in close proximity to drone stations – the furthest delivery has been around 15 km. But in the near future, particularly when batteries with better lifespans emerge, it is hoped it will hugely reduce the cost of carrying out deliveries to remote and difficult-to-reach regions of the country, which are hard to access by trucks. As well as making deliveries to customers, they will also move goods from warehouse to warehouse, which is usually done by trucks.

Speaking of trucks, JD.com is of course automating those as well. Autonomous truck vehicles deployed by the company have accumulated 17,000 hours of road driving experience, and are already used in some circumstances to make deliveries. At the moment, although the vehicles can handle open road driving just fine, a human driver has to be present to take over when it enters a city. President of the company's X-Business division, Xiao Jun, has said: "There isn't much value if our technology can only cut three drivers down to two or even one. We hope the truck is unmanned."[6]

Facial Recognition Technology

JD.com's interest in facial recognition technology revolves around its usefulness for customers proving their identification. It will be used to allow customers to make purchases simply by picking up items in its physical stores, as well as to verify their identification to get automated delivery agents to hand over their packages at their doorsteps.

Customers start by signing up through their smartphones, and using their cameras to upload high-definition detailed images of their faces, which can then be identified, even if viewed from different angles, thanks to machine learning, which can predict how the face would appear from any viewpoint. Facial recognition is generally considered to be more secure than other biometric identification techniques such as fingerprinting, which in practice can be duplicated and forged relatively easily.

Smart Fridges

As is the case with its US competitors such as Amazon, JD.com is also branching out into developing and marketing AI-equipped "smart" consumer goods.

In JD.com's case, it is specifically looking at refrigerators, and it has announced a "smart fridge" that uses cameras equipped with image recognition technology. The cameras scan items in the fridge and can even tell when they are starting to pass their expiry date. It keeps users informed via a smartphone app that can be used to place orders for items that are starting to run low.[7]

With China's population growing more wealthy and interested in the benefits of healthy eating, devices like the smart fridge sold by JD.com, as well as rivals including Alibaba and Baidu, could also make health-based suggestions on what their owners should be eating more or less of, as well as suggest healthy recipes that can be put together from the items at hand.

Smart Shops

Unlike competitors such as Amazon and Alibaba, which started out on the internet, JD.com started out with a bricks-and-mortar store in Shanghai, China, before moving online in 2014. With an ongoing interest in offline retail, it has launched its first human-free shop at its Beijing headquarters. Here, humans can pay for their purchases with a simple glance at a camera, which registers their identity through facial recognition algorithms and deducts payment from their account. Another human-less store was opened in Jakarta, Indonesia, in 2018.[8]

The technology is already being trialed in its network of grocery stores, which focus on selling fresh food items. It has announced plans to open 1,000 more of these 7Fresh branded stores to feed the country's growing appetite for healthy eating. AI is used at every level, from deciding where to put stores based on the demographics of residents, to maintaining stock levels and ensuring a steady supply of whatever happens to be in demand.[9] Smart screens are also used in the stores, which are able to display bespoke advertising to customers based on their gender and age as determined by facial recognition technology.[10]

Key Challenges, Learning Points And Takeaways

- JD.com's founder has said that he hopes to see his company's human staff reduced from 160,000 to 80,000 within the next 10 years.[11] While he says many will be retrained, it seems retaining human jobs comes secondary to driving efficiencies and improving customer experience.

- Driving efficiency within its operations and supply chain is JD.com's primary motivation for rolling out AI. Automated warehouses, delivery networks and retail outlets all form a part of this plan.

- JD.com has also partnered with social media providers to allow them to use data on their customers for AI-driven precision marketing campaigns carried out entirely through their social apps.

- Starting out as a bricks-and-mortar retailer, JD.com is blurring the boundaries between online and offline shopping through a drive to introduce e-commerce technology into its physical stores.

Notes

1. YouTube, Richard Liu, JD.com Founder, Chairman and CEO: https://www.youtube.com/watch?v=VTSKy9E3tcU&feature=youtu.be
2. Axiom, In China, A Picture of How Warehouse Jobs Can Vanish: https://www.axios.com/china-jd-warehouse-jobs-4-employees-shanghai-d19f5cf1-f35b-4024-8783-2ba79a573405.html
3. JD.com, Preparing JD.com Orders for Same Day Delivery: https://jdcorporateblog.com/gallery/preparing-jd-com-orders-day-delivery/
4. Digital Commerce 360, JD.com and Baidu Partner on Data-Powered Precision Advertising and Marketing: https://www.digitalcommerce360.com/2017/08/17/jd-com-baidu-partner-data-powered-precision-advertising-marketing/
5. Wired, Inside JD.com, the giant Chinese firm that could eat Amazon alive: https://www.wircd.co.uk/article/china-jd-ecommerce-store-delivery-drones-amazon
6. South China Morning Post, JD.com unveils self-driving truck in move to automate logistics operations: https://www.scmp.com/tech/innovation/article/2148420/jdcom-unveils-self-driving-truck-move-automate-logistics-operations
7. Medium, Why China's No.2 e-commerce site JD sees smart refrigerators as a key to IoTs boom: https://medium.com/act-news/why-chinas-no-2-e-commerce-site-jd-sees-smart-refrigerators-as-a-key-to-iots-boom-d9674a8c9a45
8. Retail Tech News, Weekly Focus: JD.Com Opens Unmanned Store in Indonesia: https://www.retailtechnews.com/2018/08/08/weekly-focus-jd-com-opens-unmanned-store-in-indonesia/
9. The Drum, JD.com expands 7FRESH stores across China as it takes on Alibaba's Hema stores: https://www.thedrum.com/news/2018/09/

24/jdcom-expands-7fresh-stores-across-china-it-takes-alibabas-hema-stores

10. Afr.com, AI Inside JD: https://www.afr.com/technology/how-chinese-ecommerce-player-jdcom-is-becoming-an-ai-powerhouse-20180719-h12vph

11. YouTube, Richard Liu, JD.com Founder, Chairman and CEO: https://www.youtube.com/watch?v=VTSKy9E3tcU&feature=youtu.be

9
MICROSOFT

Making Artificial Intelligence Part Of The Fabric Of Everyday Life

Microsoft is a US-based, multinational technology company. As one of the world's most valuable companies it focuses on areas including computer software, consumer electronics, video gaming, cloud computing and social media.

Microsoft's business model has revolved around bringing technology to the masses. Its operating systems helped make computers in homes and small businesses truly useful for millions of people. And its office productivity tools elevated the understanding of spreadsheets, databases and presentation software among the wider population. With projects such as Internet Explorer and its .Net framework, it was also a key player in opening up the world of information we have at our fingertips, thanks to the modern internet.

Microsoft's artificial intelligence (AI) strategy is built along this same guiding principle. CEO Satya Nadella has spoken about "democratizing AI"[1] – which means not just giving as many people as possible access to its benefits, but ensuring they have a say in the future of its development.

With this aim in mind, Microsoft provides tools for developers to create their own AI applications through its Azure Cognitive Services platform. Microsoft's vision is that business trends involving AI will follow a similar path as they did with the internet – eventually everyone will be on board – but they believe the effects on business and society could be even more profound.[2]

How Does Microsoft Use Artificial Intelligence?

Following the path it carved with Office and Word, Microsoft's goal is to give businesses tools they can use to deploy AI in their organizations.

At its most basic level, this could simply mean taking advantage of the AI tools contained in Office 365. PowerPoint is capable of giving design tips based on how it observes the user working, and Word uses AI to suggest meanings, alternative phrases and to check spelling, grammar and punctuation. A feature called Acronyms even works to decipher the irritating abbreviations and shorthand that can build up around an organization. It does this by analyzing emails and internal documents to understand specific language traits, and provide automated translations.[3]

Azure Cognitive Services offers "pre-built" machine learning solutions for speech recognition, text analysis, computer vision and language translation. The idea is that anyone who has an idea about how their business could use AI to get value from its data can jump in without having to be an expert in AI.

They will of course need some idea about how data can be used to drive growth and the key technologies, so to help with this, Microsoft offers an online AI School. This is a collection of resources that covers the basics of what AI can do and how to start using it.[4]

Microsoft is even trying to make it easy for us to build our own robots. Their school offers courses on the open source Robotic Operating System and the robot simulator Gazebo, as well as instructions on integrating it with Azure Cognitive Services to build truly smart, self-learning robots.[5]

Another tool that has the potential to be very useful is Sketch2Code, which is capable of generating working HTML websites from simple sketches. It uses computer vision to understand hand-drawn sketches and transform them into wireframes and working websites. It was trained on thousands of images of hand-drawn page design elements such as buttons and text boxes, as well as hand-written data.[6]

Underwater Data Centers

Cloud-based AI requires a lot of network bandwidth, and putting it in the hands of everybody means that everybody needs access to the bandwidth. To tackle this challenge, Microsoft is trialing Project Natick, which involves submerging data centers under the ocean close to coastal cities. The submersible data centers are the size of shipping containers and fully self-contained, so they can operate autonomously for years without causing any pollution.[7] As 50% of us live near a coast, the idea has the potential to bring about a quantum leap in home internet speeds.

Who Uses Microsoft Artificial Intelligence?

Microsoft Face API is a facial recognition system that is used by Uber to verify the identity of its drivers when they sign into their system to work. Drivers are required to periodically update their photo, and the Azure computer vision algorithm has to be able to match identities of millions of drivers in a fraction of a second. This gives customers peace of mind that the person driving them is who they say they are.[8]

Microsoft also works with the Renault Formula One team to build machine learning simulators that analyze every aspect of their F1 cars' performance on the circuit. The cars use an array of over 200 sensors to send data on everything from tyre wear to the condition of the track and temperature readings from the engine to Azure cloud servers. There, machine learning algorithms draw out insights that can be used to create more accurate simulations and improve racing performance.[9]

But as we established, Microsoft wants to give smaller businesses the power to use AI too. One interesting project is their work with Spektacom, a sports technology company formed by former Indian cricket captain Anil Kumble. Their technology uses Azure to interpret data from a tiny sensor weighing around 5 grams, which can be attached to a cricket bat. The aim is both to give coaches access to more accurate data on how players perform and to enable more engaging stats and interactivity for fans.[10] The plan is to roll the sensor and analytics technology out into other sports.

Bonsai

This year Microsoft acquired start-up Bonsai, which specializes in a semi-unsupervised form of machine learning known as reinforcement learning. Bonsai has developed proprietary methods for deep reinforcement learning, which Microsoft says will become the "brains" of its new autonomous systems. Bonsai has been noted for its work building intelligent systems that can be used for programming industrial control systems.

According to Microsoft, the system allows someone with experience in industrial control system programming, but no AI experience, to program a machine 30 times more quickly than they could through conventional methods.[11]

Key Challenges, Learning Points And Takeaways

- Microsoft boss Satya Nadella's vision is that AI will eventually become simply a part of the fabric of everyday life – much like computers and the internet have done.

- To achieve this his company is building tools and services that let other businesses carry out machine learning through their Azure cloud infrastructure.

- It also includes AI functionality in its mainstream office productivity software, which is already used by millions, providing tools to make jobs quicker and easier with help from machine learning.

- Microsoft has partnered with businesses of all shapes and sizes to roll out AI solutions and is now diving into reinforcement learning with its acquisition of Bonsai.

Notes

1. Microsoft, Democratizing AI: Satya Nadella on AI vision and societal impact at DLD: https://news.microsoft.com/europe/2017/01/17/democratizing-ai-satya-nadella-shares-vision-at-dld/
2. Microsoft, Microsoft AI: Empowering transformation: https://blogs.microsoft.com/ai-for-business/2018/10/11/microsoft-ai-empowering-transformation/
3. Redmond Magazine, Office 365 Gets Serious About Artificial Intelligence: https://redmondmag.com/articles/2018/02/16/office-365-gets-serious-about-ai.aspx
4. Microsoft, AI School: https://aischool.microsoft.com/en-us/home
5. Microsoft, Intelligent Robotics: https://www.ailab.microsoft.com/experiments/f508a96d-3255-474b-a769-d5b2cf2bb9d6
6. Alphr, Microsoft's AI-powered Sketch2Code builds websites and apps from drawings: http://www.alphr.com/microsoft/1009840/microsofts-ai-sketch2code-builds-websites
7. Microsoft, Project Natick: https://natick.research.microsoft.com/

8. Microsoft, Uber boosts platform security with the Face API, part of Microsoft Cognitive Services: http://customers.microsoft.com/en-US/story/uber
9. Microsoft, Renault Sport Formula One Team uses data to make rapid changes for an even faster race car: https://customers.microsoft.com/en-US/story/renault-sport-formula-one-team-discrete-manufacturing
10. The Seattle Times, Cricket pro teams with Microsoft for a bat that can track analytics in real-time, and send them to fans: https://www.seattletimes.com/business/microsoft/microsoft-partners-with-professional-cricketer-to-make-smart-bat-technology/
11. Bonsai, Bonsai Sets State-of-the-Art Reinforcement Learning Benchmark for Programming Industrial Control Systems: https://bons.ai/blog/rl-benchmark

10
TENCENT

Using Artificial Intelligence To Power WeChat And Healthcare

Tencent is a Chinese multinational internet-services and technology conglomerate. Today, Tencent's success in gaming and social media has made it one of the most valuable technology companies in the world. It is probably best known for its WeChat app, a mobile messenger service with social, picture sharing and pay functions. It's the largest social media platform in the world, with over 1 billion active monthly users.

Tencent has a huge number of interests stretching across industries from banking and real estate to space exploration and healthcare, but its focus is always the application of new technology. It is particularly prominent in the gaming and entertainment fields. This is probably why the motto of Tencent AI Lab is "Make AI Everywhere".[1]

How Does Tencent Use Artificial Intelligence?

Tencent invests aggressively in artificial intelligence (AI) start-ups when it finds technology that can drive efficiency in any of its myriad business activities. In 2017, it made the highest number of US AI-related investment deals of any of the Chinese giants.[2]

It has particularly stood out for the advancements it has made in facial recognition technology. This is so advanced that in three Chinese provinces, citizens are allowed to verify their identity through WeChat digital ID cards, rather than having to carry physical cards.[3]

The technology is also used in its video games. Amid public concern in China that prolonged gameplaying is having a detrimental effect on the health and education of children, Tencent is trialling technology that can determine if a gameplayer is under age by asking them to undergo an automated on-camera check. Once the service is live, players who refuse to take part or fail the algorithm's checks could be blocked from the game.[4]

It has also trained software "robots" to become so good at the strategy game Starcraft 2 that it can beat the computer team's AI bots on their highest difficulty setting. The interesting point here is that the computer team bots aren't really artificially intelligent in the sense we are interested in for the purpose of this book. They aren't controlled by self-learning algorithms but are simply programmed to repeatedly win – often by cheating.

Tencent's AI bots were able to challenge the Starcraft "AI" and defeat it by mimicking the tactics of the best human players. The system studied visual data from historic games, ingesting images at a rate of 16,000 frames per second, for two days, after which it was capable of defeating the computer AI at its highest level.[5]

Robots And Autonomy

Tencent has a strong interest in consumer robotics. In 2018, it led a round of investment in start-up UBtech, which specialises in robots for the home.[6] As well as building bipedal robots that can move around in a human-like fashion and even negotiate stairs, it offers a range of machines that can fill various care, entertainment, companionship and home security functions.

It's also developing self-driving cars, cashier-less shops and home assistant speaker devices, in line with its competitors at home, Alibaba and Baidu, and in the United States, Amazon and Google.

Medical Technology

Where its work stands out above that of others, however, is in its application of AI in the medical field.

Tencent has integrated its phenomenally popular WeChat messaging platform with booking systems at 38,000 healthcare facilities. This means customers can use the app to book appointments online, as well as pay for their treatment through WeChat's payment systems.[7]

It has also partnered with the start-up iCarbonX, which uses genomics and advanced scanning technology to build up the most detailed digital models yet of individual humans, gathering data that will be invaluable in the development of precision medicines.[8]

This gives it access to a huge dataset logging patient interactions with the medical institutions which it can use to train machine learning models to predict demand for treatment across the country.

It also has a system that uses machine learning and computer vision to monitor the progress of Parkinson's disease, using only video footage of the patient. By measuring the patient's movements on camera, it can keep doctors updated on how they are progressing and assist with setting dosage levels. In many cases, this can reduce the need for patients to make hospital visits for routine check-ups for the condition.[9]

Tencent Miying – Artificial Intelligence In Hospitals

Tencent Miying is an AI medical imaging and diagnosing platform that Tencent has deployed in 10 hospitals in China, with agreements in place to extend to 100 more.[10]

It is comprised of two main systems – one that uses computer vision to assist doctors with the study of medical imaging such as MRI and X-ray scans, and one that assists with diagnosing and prescribing treatment.[11]

Miying is a product developed internally in Tencent's AI labs, and employs deep learning to power image recognition algorithms trained on thousands of scans. By learning to spot correlations between anomalies, which could be indicative of disease, it becomes an increasingly valuable tool to ease the workload of doctors in a country where they are in serious shortage.[12]

After completing analysis of its scans, the second AI function applies deep learning trained on thousands of medical documents and case notes to assist with diagnosing the patient and prescribing treatment.

The AI is trained to simulate the approach a doctor would take to study the data, although it is capable of doing it far more quickly and consistently. It can identify symptoms of more than 700 diseases.[13]

Key Challenges, Learning Points And Takeaways

- Tencent is one of China's largest investors in AI and a business that continuously looks for opportunities to capitalise on AI across all of the industries in which it operates.

- Its natural language processing, image recognition and machine learning technologies are all considered world leading, and expanding their use across its partner base and subsidiaries is a key business objective.

- Its technology has huge implications for gaming in particular, where it can be used to verify identities and also create new gameplay challenges for players.

- Tencent has also been recognised in particular for its success with building AI into healthcare systems, helping surgeries and hospitals to run smoothly, and assisting doctors with diagnosing and treating illness.

Notes

1. Tencent, Tencent AI Lab: https://ai.tencent.com/ailab/index.html
2. CB Insights, Rise Of China's Big Tech In AI: What Baidu, Alibaba, And Tencent Are Working On: https://www.cbinsights.com/research/china-baidu-alibaba-tencent-artificial-intelligence-dominance/
3. CB Insights, Rise Of China's Big Tech In AI: What Baidu, Alibaba, And Tencent Are Working On: https://www.cbinsights.com/research/china-baidu-alibaba-tencent-artificial-intelligence-dominance/
4. SCMP, Tencent employs facial recognition to detect minors in top-grossing mobile game Honour of Kings: https://www.scmp.com/tech/big-tech/article/2166447/tencent-employs-facial-recognition-detect-minors-top-grossing-mobile
5. The Next Web, https://thenextweb.com/artificial-intelligence/2018/09/20/tencent-created-ai-agents-that-can-beat-starcraft-2s-cheater-ai/
6. Financial Times, Tencent drives China artificial intelligence push: https://www.ft.com/content/3143d482-4fc8-11e8-a7a9-37318e776bab
7. CB Insights, Rise Of China's Big Tech In AI: What Baidu, Alibaba, And Tencent Are Working On: https://www.cbinsights.com/research/china-baidu-alibaba-tencent-artificial-intelligence-dominance/
8. CB Insights, Lifting The Curtain On iCarbonX: China's Overnight Unicorn Is Attacking Everything From Genomics To Smart Toilets: https://www.cbinsights.com/research/icarbonx-teardown-genomics-ai-expert-research/

9. The Week, How Tencent's AI can diagnose Parkinson's disease "within minutes": http://www.theweek.co.uk/artificial-intelligence/96962/how-tencent-s-ai-can-diagnose-parkinson-s-disease-within-minutes
10. Technode, How Tencent's medical ecosystem is shaping the future of China's healthcare: https://technode.com/2018/02/11/tencent-medical-ecosystem/
11. Xinhua Finance Agency, Tencent releases first AI-aided medical platform: http://en.xfafinance.com/html/Industries/Health_Care/2018/361408.shtml
12. Economist, China Needs Many More Primary Care Doctors: https://www.economist.com/china/2017/05/11/china-needs-many-more-primary-care-doctors
13. Xinhua Finance Agency, Tencent releases first AI-aided medical platform: http://en.xfafinance.com/html/Industries/Health_Care/2018/361408.shtml

Part 2
RETAIL, CONSUMER GOODS AND FOOD AND BEVERAGE COMPANIES

11
BURBERRY

Using Artificial Intelligence To Sell Luxury

British fashion retailer Burberry sells its luxury goods online, but also through its network of over 500 bricks-and-mortar stores and concessions spread across 50 countries.[1]

In high-end fashion retail, customers still enjoy the personal touches that come with shopping in an exclusive boutique outlet. It also locates many of its outlets at airports where it caters to travelling clientele, who may need items immediately rather than delivered to their home in the near future.

Burberry's strategy for ensuring its actual stores remain competitive with virtual ones has been to bring many of the innovations made possible in the online world with web technology into the physical world – and much of this has been accomplished through artificial intelligence (AI).

What Problem Is Artificial Intelligence Helping To Solve?

Brands pushing the "luxury shopping" experience haven't been so quick to jump on board the e-commerce bandwagon as businesses aiming to replicate the day-to-day shopping experience.

Those buying expensive luxury goods clearly still appreciate being able to examine fine workmanship and high-end materials themselves before committing to buy, and enjoy being pampered in exclusive surroundings while they're doing it. This means a physical bricks-and-mortar presence in retail centers is a strategic necessity for some retailers, which is unlikely to be completely replaced by online.

Bricks-and-mortar stores still have some clear advantages over online-only outlets. Having an experienced customer service assistant on-hand is something that hasn't been fully replicated with AI yet. Although they are certainly on their way.

On the other hand, online shopping offers the convenience of not having to make a journey to the store, a world of choices and easy access to intelligent machine tools. The purpose of these tools (such as search engines) is generally to edit your potential selection down to something your human brain is capable of processing and making a decision on.

Retailers that depend on a physical storefront have the challenge of having to compete with this huge shift in choice and convenience that online retailers have brought to the game, or continue to lose customers to them.

How Is Artificial Intelligence Used In Practice?

To encourage well-heeled shoppers to keep coming into their stores, Burberry's mission has been to use advanced data technology – including AI – to replicate many of the advantages and conveniences we have come to expect online. This is chiefly carried out through a number of different loyalty programs.

Data that customers hand over is used to generate profiles and segment customers, so sales assistants can approach them with recommendations based not just on their own purchase history, but on thousands of others who fit a similar profile.

Data and AI are also used to understand why particular items may be selling well in stores but not so well online. One insight Burberry gained was the overriding importance of product images. When new images were uploaded for items that weren't selling well online, in one case sales increased by 100%.[2]

What Technology, Tools And Data Were Used?

With their customers' permission, buying habits across the group's online and physical stores are tracked, and the generated data is made available to shop assistants via a tablet terminal. This means assistants can make suggestions and show customers products they might be interested in, based on their browsing history, past purchases and even analysis of their social media.

Burberry also uses radio-frequency identification tags on in-store products to give customers insights into how they were created, and ideas about how they can be worn. This also gives Burberry more information about what the customer is interested in, in the same way that Amazon will track which products its customers browse online.

What Were The Results?

Burberry is able to quickly build a picture of who the visitors to its physical stores are, and approach them with the same convenient recommendations they would get online. Those who are accustomed to old-fashioned customer service probably appreciate interacting with a sales assistant who knows their name too!

David Harris, Burberry's senior vice president of IT, said: "We believe that AI can deliver business value through making better products, faster, cheaper processes and/or more insightful analysis."[3]

Key Challenges, Learning Points And Takeaways

- Understanding, tracking and modelling customer behavior has been a feature of offline shopping for far longer than it has with online, thanks to loyalty programs. What's new is the ability to bring advanced AI solutions to the data – technologies developed to power the e-commerce revolution.

- High-end fashion retailers need to keep a physical storefront for their discerning customers – AI can help replicate the convenience of shopping online in the real world.

Notes

1. Statistica.com, Number of Burberry stores worldwide in 2018, by outlet type: https://www.statista.com/statistics/439282/burberry-number-of-stores-worldwide-by-outlet-type/
2. Forbes, The Amazing Ways Burberry Is Using Artificial Intelligence and Big Data: https://www.forbes.com/sites/bernardmarr/2017/09/25/the-amazing-ways-burberry-is-using-artificial-intelligence-and-big-data-to-drive-success/#35325a4d4f63
3. AI Business, Where are Burberry with AI? Exclusive Interview with David Harris, SVP of IT: https://aibusiness.com/where-are-burberry-with-ai-exclusive-interview-with-david-harris-svp-of-it/

12
COCA-COLA

Using Artificial Intelligence To Stay At The Top Of The Soft Drinks Market

As the world's largest beverage company, Coca-Cola serves more than 1.9 billion drinks every day, across over 500 brands, including Diet Coke, Coke Zero, Fanta, Sprite, Dasani, Powerade, Schweppes and Minute Maid.

Big data and artificial intelligence (AI) power everything that the business does – the global director of digital innovation, Greg Chambers, said: "Artificial intelligence is the foundation for everything we do. We create intelligent experiences. Artificial intelligence is the kernel that powers that experience."[1]

What Problem Is Artificial Intelligence Helping To Solve?

Marketing soft drinks around the world is not a "one-size-fits-all affair". Coca-Cola products are marketed and sold in over 200 countries. In each of these markets there are local differences concerning flavors, sugar and calorie contents, marketing preferences and competitors faced by the brand.

This means that to stay on top of the game in every territory, it must collect and analyze huge amounts of data from disparate sources to determine which of its 500 brands are likely to be well received. The taste of their most well-known brands will even differ from country to country, and understanding these local preferences is a hugely complex task.

How Is Artificial Intelligence Used In Practice?

Coca-Cola serves a large number of its drinks every day through vending machines. On newer machines, typically the customer will interact through a touch-screen display, enabling them to select the product they want and even customize it with "shots" of different flavours. The company has begun fitting these machines with AI algorithms allowing them to promote drinks and flavors that are most likely to be well received in the specific locations where they are installed.[2]

The vending machines can even alter their "mood" depending on where they are located – with machines in a shopping mall displaying a colourful, fun persona, those in a gym more focused on achieving performance, and those in a hospital appearing more functional.

Coca-Cola also uses AI to analyze social media and understand where, when and how its customers like to consume its products, as well as which products are popular in particular localities. With over 90% of consumers making purchasing decisions based on social media content,[3] understanding how its billions of customers are discussing and interacting with the brand on platforms like Facebook, Twitter and Instagram is essential to its marketing strategy. To do this, Coca-Cola analyzed engagement with over 120,000 pieces of social content to understand the demographics and behavior of its customers and those discussing the products.

Another application of AI was in securing proof of purchase for the company's loyalty and reward schemes. When customers were asked to manually enter 14-digit product codes printed on bottle caps into websites and apps to verify their purchases, uptake was understandably low due to the unwieldy nature of the operation.

To encourage more customers to engage with these schemes, Coca-Cola worked to develop image recognition technology that allows purchases to be verified by taking a single smartphone picture.

What Technology, Tools And Data Were Used?

Coca-Cola collects data on local drink preferences through the interfaces on its touch-screen vending machines – over 1 million of them are installed in Japan alone.

To understand how its products are discussed and shared on social media, the company has set up 37 "social centers" to collect data and analyze it for insights using the Salesforce platform. The aim is to create more of the content that is shown to be effective at generating positive engagement. In the past, the process of creating this content was carried out by humans; however, the company has been actively looking at developing automated systems that will create adverts and social content informed by social data.[4]

It also uses image recognition technology to target users who share pictures on social media inferring that they could be potential customers. In one example of this strategy in action, Coca-Cola targeted adverts for its Gold Peak brand of iced tea at those who posted images that suggested they enjoy iced tea, or in which the image recognition algorithms spotted logos of competing brands.[5] Once the algorithms determined that specific individuals were likely to be fans of iced tea, and active social media users who shared images with their friends, the company knows that targeting these users with adverts is likely to be an efficient use of their advertising revenue.

For purchase verification, off-the-shelf image recognition technology proved to be insufficient for reading the low-resolution dot matrix printing used to stamp product codes onto packaging. So, Coca-Cola worked to develop its own image recognition solution using Google's TensorFlow technology.[6] This used convolutional neural networks to enable machine recognition of codes that could often appear differently depending on when and where they were printed.

What Were The Results?

Analysis of the data from vending machines by AI algorithms allows Coca-Cola to more accurately understand how the buying habits of its billions of customers varies across the globe.

It uses this to inform new product decisions – for example, the decision to launch Cherry Sprite as a bottled product in the United States was taken because the data showed that this was likely to be a winning initiative.[7]

Computer vision analysis and natural language processing of social media posts, as well as deep learning-driven analysis of social engagement metrics, allows Coca-Cola to produce social advertising that is more likely to resonate with customers and drive sales of its products.

Applying TensorFlow to create convolutional neural networks enabled scanners to recognize product codes from a simple photograph, increasing customer engagement with Coca-Cola's different loyalty programs around the world.

Key Challenges, Learning Points And Takeaways

- If you sell hundreds of different products across multiple countries, perceptions and customer behavior can vary greatly from market to market. Understanding these differences helps tailor specific messages for different markets, rather than relying on a one-size-fits-all approach.

- When you're dealing with global brands, user data from social media or generated through your own systems (such as vending machines) is vast and messy. AI provides a viable method of structuring this data and drawing out insights.

- Computer vision technology such as image recognition tools can analyze millions of social media images to help a brand understand when, how and by whom its products are enjoyed.

- As well as making marketing decisions, brands that are fully invested in AI are beginning to use it for designing new products and services.

Notes

1. Venturebeat, Coca-Cola reveals AI-powered vending machine app: https://venturebeat.com/2017/07/11/coca-cola-reveals-ai-powered-vending-machine-app/
2. Digital Food and Beverage, Coca-Cola is Using AI to Put Some Fizz in Its Vending Machines: https://foodandbeverage.wbresearch.com/coca-cola-artificial-intelligence-ai-omnichannel-strategy-ty-u
3. Nastel, Social Media Analytics At Coca-Cola: Learning From The Best: https://www.nastel.com/blog/social-media-analytics-coca-cola-learning-best/
4. Adweek, Coca-Cola Wants to Use AI Bots to Create Its Ads: https://www.adweek.com/digital/coca-cola-wants-to-use-ai-bots-to-create-its-ads/
5. Digiday, How Coca-Cola targeted ads based on people's Facebook, Instagram photos: https://digiday.com/marketing/coca-cola-targeted-ads-based-facebook-instagram-photos/
6. Google Developers Blog, How Machine Learning with TensorFlow Enabled Mobile Proof-Of-Purchase at Coca-Cola: https://developers.googleblog.com/2017/09/how-machine-learning-with-tensorflow.html

7. Coca-Cola, Fountain Favorite: Sprite Cherry is First National Brand Inspired by Coca-Cola Freestyle: https://www.coca-colacompany.com/ stories/fountain-favorites-sprite-cherry-and-sprite-cherry-zero-become -first-national-brands-inspired-by-coca-cola-freestyle

13
DOMINO'S

Using Artificial Intelligence To Serve Up
Hundreds Of Thousands Of Pizzas Every Day

Domino's Pizza is the largest pizza company in the world – it sold over 300,000 pizzas every day in 2017,[1] from 48,000 stores in 85 markets.

While cooking and delivering pizzas may not immediately seem like the most tech-driven business, Domino's has consistently ensured it is harnessing new technologies as they become available. Most noticeable until now has been its drive to allow customers to order pizzas from any platform – over 60% of its sales now come through digital channels[2] and you can order pizzas through smart TVs, Facebook, Twitter, Amazon Echo, smart watches and numerous other methods – including by simply sending a pizza emoji via SMS.

Data and analytics have long played a key part in Domino's marketing strategy, and it collects vast amounts of data to understand who is ordering its pizzas and how it can improve its service. Now it is embracing artificial intelligence (AI) to ensure a more consistent quality and build a speedier, more environmentally friendly delivery infrastructure.

What Problems Is Artificial Intelligence Helping To Solve?

In the fast food business, customers are fickle creatures. New options are regularly becoming available as habits and food fashions change, and if pizzas are cooked or delivered that do not meet their expectations in terms of consistency and quality, customers will become dissatisfied. This means they are likely to look to new alternatives and rival businesses for their fast food fix.

And while pizza delivery may be a very convenient way of getting fed from a customer's point of view, it is an expensive exercise – in terms of both fuel and wages, which the company has to cover, and the environmental cost of making an individual journey to deliver each pizza.

How Is Artificial Intelligence Used In Practice?

Domino's has started using a system called Pizza Checker that photographs every pizza when it leaves the oven, and then uses machine learning algorithms to inspect it for quality before it reaches the hungry customer.[3]

The camera system checks the type of pizza against the customer's order to make sure they are getting what they paid for. It also verifies that toppings are distributed evenly and that the crust has been properly baked at the correct temperature.

The system – installed in 2,000 Domino's kitchens in seven countries in 2017 – sends users a picture of their pizza before it is delivered, and also notifies them if a quality failure meant that the pizza had to be remade. The hope here is that this will make them more understanding when there are occasionally inevitable delays!

AI is also used when processing customer orders received over the telephone. It has developed its own "virtual assistant" technology in the style of Apple's Siri, which can communicate with customers by voice when they call to place an order. The first iteration of this technology was launched in 2014 and is known as Dom. Last year, a new version – called DRU (Domino's Robotic Unit)[4] – was rolled out, featuring more sophisticated natural language processing technology.

This means it can respond to more complex queries and understand the sometimes very different speech patterns and mannerisms used by different callers.

DRU is actually the name used for the company's autonomous technology across all of its units, including the pizza checkers, virtual ordering assistants and its autonomous delivery vehicles.

Yes, Domino's is also actively working to make self-driving pizza delivery a reality. Thanks to a partnership with Ford, pizza lovers in Ann Arbor[5] and Miami,[6] USA, have been able to take part in an experiment where their pizzas are delivered by a fleet of autonomous vehicles equipped with ovens to keep the pizzas warm during their journey. In their initial trial, the vehicles had to be accompanied by humans.

More recently, the company has been launching completely autonomous delivery pilots in Germany and the Netherlands, where it is partnering with Starship Technologies.[7] Don Meij, Domino's Group CEO and Managing Director, says: "We are a global company and we are eager to progress innovative technology in all of the countries in which we operate – we are very excited to be partnering with Starship as it brings regular deliveries by robot one step closer to commercial operations."

What Technology, Tools And Data Were Used?

Domino's Pizza Checker has been developed by Dragontail Systems and uses Google image recognition algorithms to identify the type and placement of toppings on a pizza, as well as the temperature that the pizza was cooked at. It uses data from the customers' orders to ensure the right pizza is being prepared. This is done using computer vision technology, which allows AI algorithms to be trained to "see" – and recognise objects in the same way humans do.

As for autonomous delivery – Domino's has partnered with Starship Technologies to use delivery robots that are capable of guiding themselves to customers' homes. The six-wheeled Starship bots use GPS, radar, ultrasonic sensors, as well as cameras to navigate autonomously. The customers will then be able to access the compartments where their food is kept hot, and the drinks are kept cold, by using a smartphone app.

What Were The Results?

Domino's hopes that the computer vision system will lead to fewer pizzas being rejected because they don't meet customers' quality expectations. In worst case scenarios, this can lead to customers who otherwise have high lifetime value expectations to the chain taking their custom elsewhere.

This year the business announced that it will invest a further $1 million in fitting its kitchens out with the automated camera systems provided by Dragontail.[8]

And although Domino's has said that the DRU delivery vehicle won't be appearing at customers' doorsteps "tomorrow", it fully anticipates that autonomous delivery will become a reality in the near future.

Key Challenges, Learning Points And Takeaways

- When you have huge numbers of outlets serving millions of customers, those customers will come to expect a level of consistency of the quality of products and service. AI can help maintain that level.

- Companies like Domino's believe that natural language technology is at a stage where it can provide the same level of customer service as a human telephone operator.

- As well as moving people around, autonomous vehicles have applications for moving goods from place to place, and even delivering them straight to customers' doors. As well as saving the operators' money (which can be passed onto the customers with lower prices), this could have positive environmental benefits as robots will be able to route themselves more efficiently than humans.

Notes

1. The Times, Pizza guzzlers give Domino's a slice of success: https://www.thetimes.co.uk/article/pizza-guzzlers-give-dominos-a-slice-of-success-dzftlldtn
2. PR Newswire, Domino's on Quest for Digital Dominance Using Artificial Intelligence: https://www.prnewswire.com/news-releases/dominos-on-quest-for-digital-dominance-using-artificial-intelligence-300633827.html
3. Interesting Engineering, Domino's Will Use AI to Make Sure Every Pizza They Serve Is Perfect: https://interestingengineering.com/dominos-will-use-ai-to-make-sure-every-pizza-they-serve-is-perfect
4. ZDNet, Domino's partners with Nuance for DRU artificial intelligence: https://www.zdnet.com/article/dominos-partners-with-nuance-for-dru-artificial-intelligence/
5. Tech Radar, Ford and Domino's are filling self-driving cars with pizza to see how we feel about it: https://www.techradar.com/news/ford-and-

dominos-are-filling-self-driving-cars-with-pizza-to-see-how-we-feel-about-it
6. Tech Radar, Ford and Domino's demonstrate self-driving deliveries with – what else – pizza: https://www.techradar.com/news/ford-and-dominos-demonstrate-self-driving-deliveries-with-what-else-pizza
7. Starship, https://www.starship.xyz/press_releases/starship-technologies-launches-pilot-program-with-dominos-pizza-enterprises/
8. Domino's Pizza moves forward with Dragontail Systems AI: https://www.finnewsnetwork.com.au/archives/finance_news_network190563.html

14
KIMBERLY-CLARK

Using AI To Make Sense Of Customer Data

Kimberly-Clark produces some of the world's best-known personal care brands, including Huggies, Kleenex and Scott, which are sold in 175 countries. In fact, one in four of the world's population uses its products on a regular basis.[1]

While its products may not be the most glamorous, they are an essential part of day-to-day life, meaning huge amounts of resources are spent to ensure they are effectively produced, sold and distributed.

This means, like many other large businesses, Kimberly-Clark has found that the most productive way forward has been to essentially become a technology company. As well as producing the everyday goods it has built its name on, it licenses over 150 of its self-built technologies to other businesses, ranging from start-ups to Fortune 100 companies.[2]

What Problems Is Artificial Intelligence Helping To Solve?

In Kimberly-Clark's market, businesses need to build intimate understandings of their customers' lives to understand how they interact with their products.

This means understanding how life-changing events like pregnancy and weddings will affect their buying habits and patterns.

To do this, they have to make as much sense as they can out of the explosion of data customers leave behind as they browse their product websites and social channels or make purchases in stores. Even with computers this was a monumental challenge, before artificially intelligent software solutions started to become available in recent years.

As well as this, Kimberly-Clark faces a challenge common to all businesses looking to undergo digital transformation. The one ingredient that is still essential to staying ahead of the tech curve is people. Machine learning is great, but it hasn't quite reached the stage where it's capable of the blue sky/out-of-the-box (insert your own cliché!) thinking necessary for coming up with brilliant new ideas.

The people who are good at it are in very high demand – global demand for trained data scientists was said to outstrip supply by 50% in 2018,[3] and this is predicted to grow. Considering their options, working for a company primarily known for producing toilet paper and diapers might not be the most obvious career path for these talented people.

How Is Artificial Intelligence Used In Practice?

Kimberly-Clark uses artificial intelligence (AI) to make sense of all of the data it gathers from customers and its business operations.

This data is used to build detailed models of who its customers are. Actual customers can then be "segmented" according to which model they fit best, to give the business clues about what they might want to buy.

One key success has been the increase in accuracy with predicting when customers would fall pregnant. Research showed that introducing them to the Huggies brand as early as possible to their finding out they were pregnant was key to converting them into a customer for the duration of their pregnancy. Once identified as likely to be shopping for pregnancy-related items, customers could be encouraged to sign up for loyalty schemes, and could be offered discount coupons, as well as useful content such as baby care advice.[4]

What Technology, Tools And Data Were Used?

Worldwide over 15,000 Kimberly-Clark products are sold every second of every day. Each one of those sales generates data points, ranging from time and place of sale to customer information from loyalty schemes or online shopping profiles, as well as external data from sources such as Nielsen ratings.

With so much data, traditional business intelligence and customer relations technology can't operate quickly enough to produce insights before the data becomes obsolete.

AI and the technology, which has built up to support it – big data platforms like Hadoop and Internet of Things frameworks – make it possible to extract meaning from the madness.

Kimberly-Clarke has partnered with Nielsen to use its Marketing Cloud platform and RevTrax software, as well as solutions from Webtrends, which use machine learning to offer promotions and provide tailored customer experiences.[5] It involves using predictive analytics to understand what segment customers fit into, and offer them relevant products (such as diapers in the Huggies example).

Other partnerships it sees working are Tableau, Amazon and Panopoly to store and sort through the mountains of data it collects.[6]

In this example of targeted marketing, data would be collected by showing different social promotions and content marketing material to differently segmented audience samples. This is what marketers have always traditionally done with focus groups. But a machine learning solution working across social media can test against different target audiences far more quickly than a human-organized focus group ever could. This means Kimberly-Clark can break customers down into precisely defined groups, and build more accurate models of what potential customers look like, for particular products, at any given time.

Kimberly-Clark also hosts the K-Challenge to persuade rising stars in the world of data science and AI tech to consider building their career in the personal hygiene products arena.

The competitive event encourages innovators to submit their ideas for consumer goods technology. Kimberly-Clarke offers support for the chosen winners with research and design, marketing and making the idea into a reality.[7]

What Were The Results?

Kimberly-Clark's move towards advanced analytics with Webtrends resulted in increased sign-up rates of 17%.

Another campaign, to optimize targeting of customers for their Depend brand, saw a 24% increase in conversions.[8]

This was done by producing content that more closely aligned with the customer profiles that the analytics predicted would be responsive. These customers are also more likely to go on to be long-term repeat buyers, as well as to make positive recommendations to friends and family.

Key Challenges, Learning Points And Takeaways

- Today, market-leading companies in every industry are transitioning into tech companies – it's essential if they want to stay ahead of the pack.

- AI-driven analytics is far more powerful than traditional business intelligence solutions for customer segmentation and targeting when dealing with truly big data.

- Businesses must earn their reputations as tech champions and pioneers to attract the necessary human talent. Until computers are clever enough to start running corporations on their own, of course.

Notes

1. Kimberly-Clark, https://www.kimberly-clark.com/cn-us/brands/our-brands
2. Kimberly-Clark, https://www.kimberly-clark.com/en-us/company/technology-licensing
3. Inside Big Data, https://insidebigdata.com/2018/08/19/infographic-data-scientist-shortage/
4. Webtrends, https://www.webtrends.com/about-us/client-success/kimberly-clark/
5. Nielsen, Machine Learning Powered Marketing Personalization Innovation: https://www.nielsen.com/us/en/press-room/2016/machine-learning-powered-marketing-personalization-innovation-unveiled.html
6. Tableau, How Kimberly-Clark saved $250k with a platform powered by Tableau, Amazon Redshift, and Panoply: https://www.tableau.com/about/blog/2018/2/how-kimberly-clark-saved-250k-platform-powered-tableau-amazon-redshift-and-panoply
7. KC Lab, http://kcdlab.com/
8. Webtrends, https://www.webtrends.com/about-us/client-success/kimberly-clark/

15
MCDONALD'S

Using Robots And Artificial Intelligence To Automate Processes

McDonald's employs 400,000 staff across its 36,000 restaurants spread over 120 countries.[1]

At the start of 2017, it unveiled a new strategy[2] focused on using digital technology, including artificial intelligence (AI), to drive growth.

Self-service kiosks are increasingly prominent in its outlets, and are often cited as one of the more visible signs of a trend towards replacing human workers with machines.

However, in the company's own words, its main drive is to use technology for "re-shaping our interactions with the customer – whether they eat in, take out, drive thru or order delivery".

What Problem Is Artificial Intelligence Helping To Solve?

Restaurant chains have to carefully manage their inventories to avoid unsold food going to waste or items not being in stock when customers want them.

Traditional, static menu displays don't offer the flexibility to allow stores to promote items most likely to appeal at different times of the day unless they are manually updated.

On top of that, McDonald's restaurants often attract large volumes of customers at peak times during the day. While this is largely what has made the brand the success it is, dealing with large numbers of people all expecting to be served very quickly and accurately is challenging in its own right.

How Is Artificial Intelligence Used In Practice?

Rather than just being straightforward terminals, those McDonald's self-service kiosks that have sprung up around the world in recent years, as well as the digital menu boards used in stores, are equipped with smart, analytic technology.

This means that decisions can be made autonomously at restaurant level about what to promote and sell to customers. This decision is based on factors including local ordering trends, the weather and what inventory the restaurant needs to shift before it goes out of date.[3]

The menus can intelligently adapt too, for example, begin to offer more hearty, warming comfort food items when the temperature drops. While on sunny days, salads and ice creams will be given prominence on the displays.

McDonald's also offers an app that lets users create an account and place orders directly from their phone. This gives it access to data that is used to offer exclusive deals to customers it predicts will be interested.

It also allows it to build aggregated datasets showing what the most popular purchases are across different locations among different seg-mented customer groups.

What Technology, Tools And Data Were Used?

McDonald's self-service kiosks are already installed at all of its restaurants in the United Kingdom and Canada. In the United States it is installing 1,000 self-service kiosks per quarter and they will be in every restaurant by 2020.[4]

The company has said very little about the exact data that is collected and used, but Intel states that the terminals help the company "collect data and learn about customer behavior".[5]

It is likely that it uses this data to predict what customers are likely to buy, based on other orders that fit a similar pattern, both in terms of what was bought, and external factors such as the time of day and the restaurant's location.

McDonald's is far from the only fast food chain switching over to self-service kiosks and it is very likely to be keeping a keen eye on what its competitors are doing with the technology.

For example, KFC in Beijing has partnered with Baidu to fit kiosks with facial recognition technology, which uses AI to predict what menu items a customer is likely to be interested in, based not only on their age and sex, but also their mood. Items that match those ordered by people with similar profiles are displayed most prominently on the screen.[6] The chicken chain plans to roll these screens out to 5,000 of their restaurants, and if results are positive McDonald's will be keen to follow in their footsteps.

And it isn't just front-of-house jobs that are being automated in the fast food industry. US chain Caliburger is trialling a robotic kitchen assistant called Flippy, which uses cloud-based AI along with thermal vision that enables it to "see" how well a burger is cooked on the inside.[7]

What Were The Results?

Customers get to skip lines when they arrive to pick up their order, and benefit from spending less time browsing menus to find the items they want.

In return, McDonald's collects detailed information about their behavior, which it can use to predict future buying patterns.

In Canada where stores were first fitted with the digital, predictive menu boards, sales increased overall by 3 to 3.5% in their first year.[8]

And in Japan, users of the mobile phone app spend on average 35% more per transaction, which McDonald's attributes to presentation of individually chosen promotions.[9]

So, what about the social implications? Are their terminals and apps the visible signs of a move by big businesses to replace humans with machines?

Well, if it leads to a sustainable reduction in costs (and it hasn't yet been proven that it will), the answer is unfortunately likely to be yes – in the long term, at least.

It's possible that politicians could step in and stop this from happening or mitigate against its effects. Some seem to have the issue in their sights, for example, Jeremy Corbyn, leader of the UK Labour Party, who has called for a "robot tax".[10]

His argument is that corporations benefiting from AI should be obliged to share some of the wealth they create with society, and to absorb some of the cost of the human unemployment they seem set to create.

But overall it doesn't seem to be an issue that is inspiring the strength of public opinion it often takes to get politicians to take up a cause. At least not yet … it's possible that this is a problem the public will be more aware of over time.

Of course, it's only fair to point out that McDonald's own position on the matter is that it is emphatically not replacing human staff with robots.

It says that cashiers whose jobs are made redundant by the machines will be transferred into other roles, primarily front-of-house customer service.[11] In theory, this should make their work more rewarding as well as teach them new skills, which will be useful in their own career development.

But then, they would say that, wouldn't they?

Key Challenges, Learning Points And Takeaways

- Businesses that are engaging in automation and AI are keen to imply that technology will assist workers rather than replace them.

- However, the long-term impact that the spread of intelligent automation into all business sectors will have on human job markets is still unknown.

Notes

1. Investopedia, McDonald's vs. Burger King: Comparing Business Models: https://www.investopedia.com/articles/markets/111015/mcdonalds-vs-burger-king-comparing-business-models.asp
2. McDonald's, https://corporate.mcdonalds.com/corpmcd/about-us/our-growth-strategy.html

3. Food Business News, McDonald's finds flexibility with digital menu boards: https://www.foodbusinessnews.net/articles/7624-mcdonald-s-finds-flexibility-with-digital-menu-boards

4. USA Today, McDonald's: You buy more from touch-screen kiosks than a person. So expect more kiosks: https://eu.usatoday.com/story/money/nation-now/2018/06/07/mcdonalds-add-kiosks-citing-better-sales-over-face-face-orders/681196002/

5. Intel, McDonald's And Predictive Analytics: They're Lovin' It: https://www.intel.co.uk/content/www/uk/en/it-managers/mcdonalds-predictive-analytics.html

6. The Guardian, KFC China is using facial recognition tech to serve customers – but are they buying it?: https://www.theguardian.com/technology/2017/jan/11/china-beijing-first-smart-restaurant-kfc-facial-recognition

7. Live Science, Humans Couldn't Keep Up with This Burger-Flipping Robot, So They Fired It: https://www.livescience.com/61994-flippy-burger-flipping-robot-flops.html

8. Food Business News, McDonald's finds flexibility with digital menu boards: https://www.foodbusinessnews.net/articles/7624-mcdonald-s-finds-flexibility-with-digital-menu-boards

9. Techemergence, Fast Food Robots, Kiosks, and AI Use Cases from 6 Restaurant Chain Giants: https://www.techemergence.com/fast-food-robots-kiosks-and-ai-use-cases/

10. ZDnet, Jeremy Corbyn wants to tax robots and their greedy overlords: https://www.zdnet.com/article/jeremy-corbyn-wants-to-tax-robots-and-their-greedy-overlords/

11. Business Insider, McDonald's shoots down fears it is planning to replace cashiers with kiosks: http://uk.businessinsider.com/what-self-serve-kiosks-at-mcdonalds-mean-for-cashiers-2017-6

16
SAMSUNG

Automating The Home And Workplace With Artificial Intelligence

Samsung is the world's largest consumer electronics company by revenue, manufacturing and selling 500 million connected devices every year.

In 2018 it announced that within two years, artificial intelligence (AI) will be baked into every single one of them.[1] From the latest phones to fridges, TVs and washing machines, Samsung is betting that the added convenience will drive consumer spending towards their products.

Samsung also make industrial technology, and this year the company unveiled Saram (Korean for "Person") – an AI-equipped robot that initially will be used for heavy lifting, but could end up performing surgery.

What Problems Is Artificial Intelligence Helping To Solve?

In our homes, connected devices are increasingly a part of our lives – modern cars, homes, phones and appliances are packed with data capture and sharing capabilities. The applications are endless, from fitness trackers that collect data that we can analyse on our smartphones, to electricity meters that analyse our use of power and tell us where we could cut waste.

The problem is, it's still very early days for much of this technology, and there's a messy tangle of different standards and protocols vying to become our favourite. When we have to rely on a bunch of different apps and interfaces to get at this data, our ability to correlate it and make useful sense of it can be severely hampered by information overload.

At work, too, intelligent technology and robotics are becoming commonplace. In the past they were capable of carrying out routine and boring tasks if they were diligently programmed to do so. However, abilities to carry out tasks involving even a tiny degree of deviation from the norm were severely limited until the arrival of machine learning.

How Is Artificial Intelligence Used In Practice?

Currently, Samsung has an AI personal assistant, much like Apple's Siri and Amazon's Alexa, that goes by the name of Bixby.

With so many voice-enabled virtual assistants becoming available, the differences show where companies are being innovative and where they are just going with the flow. One of Bixby's distinguishing characteristics is that it is capable of integrating throughout the entirety of an application it interfaces with.[2] With other voice systems, specific keywords are hard-linked to specific functions of the application, such as starting or stopping media playback on a music app.

It would be a good bet to say that this technology will end up underpinning Samsung's plans for all of its devices to be artificially intelligent by 2020.

What Samsung is trying to do is use AI to break down the final barriers in the way of our communication with machines. Previously, machines had to be laboriously programmed in technical programming languages. Now we are seeing a shift towards communicating in simple spoken human languages.

This revolution is taking place in industrial settings as well as homes. Samsung is already using an artificially intelligent robotic arm in manufacturing operations.

Its Saram robot AI was unveiled in 2018 and will initially be used in factories and manufacturing plants to carry out heavy lifting duties. It will be integrated into robotic arms of the type often used in high-tech manufacturing operations. However, the addition of AI to the mechanical arms will mean they are capable of working smarter, for example, spotting if parts are damaged or faulty before assembling them into a finished product.

In the future it could become part of a bipedal robot, which Samsung is reportedly also developing.[3]

Robotic factory workers could be used to carry out tasks that are dangerous or uncomfortable for humans to carry out for prolonged lengths of time.

Samsung has also invested in the Israeli robotics manufacturer Intuition Robotics.[4] Intuition has developed the "social companion" robot ElliQ, a virtual assistant designed to help and engage the elderly in their homes. This shows that Samsung is committed to its plan of rolling out its AI and robotics into people's homes.

What Technology, Tools And Data Were Used?

Samsung's Bixby voice assistant uses natural language processing to interpret what it should do based on what a person says. Like other voice assistants, it uses neural nets and deep learning to become better at understanding how we talk and what we mean. This gets over the barriers to communication caused by humans with their inferior brains having to memorise a list of exact commands and phrases the computer will understand.

This year it also launched its SmartThings app, which is a platform for unifying all of its different intelligent devices. It hopes mainstream buyers will start installing smart refrigerators, kettles and coffee makers in their homes once the process of managing them is convenient enough.

Very little has been made public knowledge about the Saram robot system, apart from a spokesman stating that it uses AI technology. Speculation based on patent and trademark applications has suggested they are working towards a human-like, bipedal robot for industrial applications. The problems inherent in creating such a robot are quickly being solved as AI brings us closer to computer-controlled motors, which can work accurately enough to ambulate a humanoid body. The latest humanoid robots can keep their balance if struck by other moving objects without warning.[5]

What Were The Results?

Bixby has enabled Samsung to compete with Amazon, Apple and Microsoft by equipping its phones with a natural language virtual assistant. Users have a more frictionless interaction with their device and ultimately can get things done more quickly and easily.

It accounted for 6.2% of the market for AI-enabled voice assistant devices sold in May 2018 – behind market leaders Siri (Apple) at 45.6% and Google Assistant at 28.7%.[6] It's worth noting that unlike Google Assistant and Siri, Bixby is only available on phones and isn't a stand-alone assistant device. But this is likely to change if Samsung's plan for all their devices to be equipped with AI by 2020 comes to fruition.

By developing the SmartThings platform, Samsung is in with a chance of becoming one of the first companies to successfully market the concept of the "connected home" to the non-techie public. With homes becoming increasingly computerised, whoever develops the operating system that becomes the standard for connecting everything together is likely to win big.

Key Challenges, Learning Points And Takeaways

- Samsung has shown it is firmly committed to the idea that AI will dominate consumer electronics with its 2020 promise.

- Samsung is also betting heavily that autonomous, mobile robots will have a huge impact in our homes and workplaces.

- Services will let us use AI to tie together all of the data we gather through disparate "smart" devices and present it to us in a way we can use to take action.

- Smart, connected homes are still the preserve of the tech-savvy slice of the population, but that's likely to change as more people become aware of the efficiencies on offer, and solutions are presented in a more consumer-friendly way.

Notes

1. Financial Review, CES 2018: Samsung vows to add artificial intelligence to everything it does: https://www.afr.com/technology/ces-2018-samsung-vows-to-add-artificial-intelligence-to-everything-it-does-20180108-h0fdtd
2. Forbes, How Is Samsung's Bixby Different From Other Voice First Systems?: https://www.forbes.com/sites/quora/2017/03/23/how-is-samsungs-bixby-different-from-other-voice-first-systems/#6ea3d30445f3

3. Business Korea, Samsung Electronics to Make Artificial Intelligence Robot "Saram": http://www.businesskorea.co.kr/news/articleView.html?idxno=20610
4. Venturebeat, Intuition Robotics nabs Samsung as investor, launches U.S. beta trial of ElliQ companion robot: https://venturebeat.com/2018/01/09/intuition-robotics-nabs-samsung-as-investor-and-launches-beta-trial-of-elliq-social-companion-robot/
5. The Week, Bipedal humanoid robot masters human balancing act: https://www.theweek.in/news/sci-tech/2018/10/03/Bipedal-humanoid-robot-masters-human-balancing-act.html
6. Business Insider, Siri owns 46% of the mobile voice assistant market – one and half times Google Assistant's share of the market: http://uk.businessinsider.com/siri-google-assistant-voice-market-share-charts-2018-6

17
STARBUCKS

Using Artificial Intelligence To Sell Millions Of Coffees Every Day

Starbucks has close to 30,000[1] outlets around the world and serves up around 4 billion cups of coffee annually.

It isn't just simple coffees though – from a classic espresso to an iced caramel mochaccino there are actually around 87,000[2] combinations available on a typical Starbucks menu!

Although the brand has long been a market leader in the United States where it was founded, in the mid-1990s it began expanding overseas into markets where it often faced strong competition from local chains. As of 2018 its biggest non-domestic market is China, where 12.4% of its branches are now located.[3]

The way coffee and tea – which make up the majority of Starbucks sales – are consumed varies across cultures. The coffee shop giant generates and burns through mountains of transactional and customer data in its attempt to offer personalized service to millions.

What Problems Is Artificial Intelligence Helping To Solve?

With so many stores offering so many products in so many parts of the world, precise calculations must be made to keep the thousands of outlets stocked and ready to serve their customers. Slight miscalculations can mean large overspends on logistics such as transport and storage. With businesses as large and broadly distributed as Starbucks, small inefficiencies very quickly add up to large ones.

Operating internationally, Starbucks is often competing with local chains and brands that are already synchronized with the lives of the customers they serve. Starbucks may offer US-style customer service to markets that have traditionally taken a more relaxed approach to serving hot drinks. But it has to adapt to local cultural norms and fit with local customers' habits if it wants to become a part of their everyday lives.

How Is Artificial Intelligence Used In Practice?

Starbucks gathers data on its customers' behavior by tracking them (with their permission) through its loyalty programs and mobile apps.

Customers can use the app to pay for food and drinks in advance before collecting them at the counter, and as of 2017 more than 17 million people were using it.[4]

This information is correlated with other internal and external data, including meteorological data, local data and company data such as inventory levels to help Starbucks understand what is driving sales.

This means that personalized promotions can be offered – offering deals on items that each customer is likely to be interested in directly to them.

The artificial intelligence (AI)-enabled system that it uses to do all of this is called the Digital Flywheel Program.[5] Its job is to take into account every factor from locality, to time of day, to weather – to predict what customers will order when they walk through the door or load up the app on their phone.

AI will also play a key part in Starbucks' move to branch out into offering delivery in China.

It has partnered with Alibaba, and will use technology developed by the retail tech giant's recent acquisition Ele.me,[6] a food delivery service that is heavily built on smart technology. In 2017, Ele.me unveiled its autonomous food delivery robot,[7] which uses machine learning to navigate as it distributes beverages and snacks. Designed to operate autonomously in large office buildings, perhaps it won't be long before we can have coffee delivered directly to our desks by robots?

Choosing to partner with Alibaba rather than develop its own delivery service in China could be a shrewd move. Alibaba (and subsidiary Ele.me) has a sophisticated delivery network in place and AI to drive efficiency. Developing these from scratch would be very expensive for Starbucks.

What Key Tools, Technology And Data Were Used?

Starbucks announced that AI would be built into its Digital Flywheel data analytics program in 2017.

Much of the data it feeds into its analytics comes from processing 90 million transactions every week through its stores and apps.[8]

This tells them everything they need to know about who is buying what, where and when. The data can then be correlated with individual customers' data gathered through loyalty programs or app use.

The app itself features AI in the form of the virtual barista feature.[9] Like other virtual assistants, this one uses natural language processing to understand the nuanced way humans talk. This one is specifically trained to adapt to the complex and evolving languages we use when ordering drinks at coffee chains.

What Were The Results?

Through better understanding its customers habits, Starbucks is able to build brand loyalty by offering the right products at the right time, and personalized promotional offers.

This means it can tailor its product range and marketing strategies towards individual markets, using localized datasets that are highly likely to be relevant.

Starbucks has said that by 2019, 80% of its stores around the world will have access to the Digital Flywheel.[10]

Key Challenges, Learning Points And Takeaways

- Working worldwide across an enormous number of markets makes getting a thorough overview of your customer base challenging, but today's machine learning technology means it can be done.

- Starbucks offers customers conveniences such as being able to order ahead and skip queues, in exchange for data it can use to improve services.

- Just as in other areas of retail, food and drink outlets are transforming in an attempt to offer online convenience. This means interactivity between mobile phones and in-store systems, and in-app purchasing.

- Partnerships are often a huge benefit when branching out in new directions. Today, partnering with tech specialists means you can share their data, analytics technology, or increasingly both, on an as-a-service basis.

Notes

1. Starbucks, How many Starbucks stores are out there?: https://www.loxcel.com/sbux-faq.html
2. Favrify, 18 Exotic Starbucks Drinks That You Didn't Know Existed…: https://www.favrify.com/starbucks-drinks/
3. Starbucks, How many Starbucks stores are out there?: https://www.loxcel.com/sbux-faq.html
4. Cio, Starbucks' CTO brews personalized experiences: https://www.cio.com/article/3050920/analytics/starbucks-cto-brews-personalized-experiences.html
5. Zacks, Starbucks' Digital Flywheel Program Will Use Artificial Intelligence: https://www.zacks.com/stock/news/270022/starbucks-digital-flywheel-program-will-use-artificial-intelligence
6. The Star, Starbucks partners with Alibaba, as it tries to keep its coffee throne in China: https://www.thestar.com/business/2018/08/02/starbucks-partners-with-alibaba-as-it-tries-to-keep-its-coffee-throne-in-china.html
7. Pandaily, Ele.me Delivery Robot Completed Takeout Delivery for the First Time: https://pandaily.com/ele-me-delivery-robot-completed-takeout-delivery-for-the-first-time/
8. Cio, Starbucks' CTO brews personalized experiences: https://www.cio.com/article/3050920/analytics/starbucks-cto-brews-personalized-experiences.html
9. Starbucks, Starbucks debuts voice ordering: https://news.starbucks.com/press-releases/starbucks-debuts-voice-ordering
10. Zdnet, Starbucks to step up rollout of "digital flywheel" strategy: https://www.zdnet.com/article/starbucks-to-step-up-rollout-of-digital-flywheel-strategy/

18
STITCH FIX

Combining The Power Of Artificial Intelligence And Humans To Disrupt Fashion Retail

Stitch Fix, founded in 2011 and based in California, USA, aims to revolutionize fashion retail by acting as a personal stylist, automatically shipping items that it thinks the customer will want to wear.

It does this by asking customers to fill in a survey stating their style preferences, budget and optionally giving the company's stylists access to their social media accounts.

The work of the stylists is augmented by data scientists and artificial intelligence (AI), which aim to provide customers with clothes they will want to wear by analyzing their preferences and comparing them with thousands of other customers who fit their profile.

What Problems Is Artificial Intelligence Helping To Solve?

The proportion of our shopping that we do online is continuing to soar – in the United Kingdom it climbed from 11.6% of total (non-food) retail spending in 2013 to 24.4 in 2017.[1]

Fashion retailers are uniquely challenged by the relatively high rate of customer returns. They are also obliged to offer both free delivery and returns to compete. This can often add up to a large expense for businesses if their customers order large quantities of clothing to assess at home and end up returning most items.

As well as the cost of shipping and processing returns, this situation can make it difficult for retailers to manage their inventories, and often requires them to be overstocked to be able to fulfil customer demand. In the fashion industry, it is normal for large quantities of clothing to be sold at greatly reduced prices, or even destroyed due to inefficient forecasting of demand.[2]

This is all hugely wasteful and, of course, eats into profits. Providing clothes to customers that will fit and meet their quality expectations, therefore minimizing returns, is a key challenge for all online fashion retailers.

How Is Artificial Intelligence Used In Practice?

Stitch Fix uses AI to understand its customers' body measurements as well as their tastes and style preferences.

These algorithms all work to augment the work of human stylists. As well as retailing, Stitch Fix designs clothes, and the concepts for new items are informed by insights into what is popular, derived from the AI analysis.

Their chief algorithm officer, Eric Colson, said: "Our business is getting relevant things into the hands of our customers. This is the one thing in the world we're going to be best at. We couldn't do this with machines alone. We couldn't do with humans alone. We're just trying to get them to combine their powers."

What Technology, Tools And Data Were Used?

A team of around 85 data scientists work with the Stitch Fix AI platform to select items for which there is a high probability that customers will want to keep the items.[3]

Colson brought machine learning with him from Netflix, where he was previously employed as vice president of data science and engineering. This technology allowed the business to greatly increase the efficiency of its algorithms that were already being used to filter out items when they would be unsuitable for a particular customer.

When signing up for an account, prospective customers are asked for their measurements, weight, style preferences (such as slim or baggy fit), colour preferences, budget, personality questions such as how adventurous their selection should be, and for specific details such as whether they often find shirts or jeans too tight or too loose.

If you give it permission, it will also take into account what it can learn about your style and preferences through social media. It will also take data it collects from every point of feedback, such as when customers fill in forms to give details about why they are returning items.

As well as matching products to clients, Stitch Fix has specific algorithms for assigning personal stylists to clients, making inventory decisions, analyzing images posted to social media (Pinterest) by clients and assessing how happy they are with the service they are receiving.[4]

What Were The Results?

The money we spend on online retail is quickly catching up with what we spend in bricks-and-mortar stores. Online retail provides unique customer service challenges, and AI has the potential to offer a plethora of solutions.

Understanding customer requirements and preferences has meant that Stitch Fix is able to automatically despatch items that, according to its data, its customers are more likely to love. This allows it to avoid wasted warehouse space, shipping costs, return expenses and end-of-season overstock.

Stitch Fix says that its adoption of machine learning has allowed it to increase revenue and customer satisfaction, while decreasing overall costs.[5]

Key Challenges, Learning Points And Takeaways

- The better understanding that AI can give you of your customer, the less chance there is that you will disappoint them with your products and services.

- AI poses a real risk to human jobs, just as all other industrial revolutions before it did. Designing intelligent systems that augment the capabilities of human workers rather than make them redundant is a key challenge across all industries. Stitch Fix's algorithms inform the work of human stylists and analysts, who have the final say. Which is probably just as well – remembering it was the weavers who were among the first to take up arms during the first industrial revolution!

Notes

1. Financial Times, Online retail sales continue to soar: https://www.ft.com/content/a8f5c780-f46d-11e7-a4c9-bbdefa4f210b

2. Fashion United, The fashion industry at a dead end: new products worth millions destroyed: https://fashionunited.uk/news/business/the-fashion-industry-at-a-dead-end-new-products-worth-millions-destroyed/2018071930847

3. ZD Net, How Stitch Fix uses machine learning to master the science of styling: https://www.zdnet.com/article/how-stitch-fix-uses-machine-learning-to-master-the-science-of-styling/

4. ComputerWorld, At Stitch Fix, data scientists and A.I. become personal stylists: https://www.computerworld.com/article/3067264/artificial-intelligence/at-stitch-fix-data-scientists-and-ai-become-personal-stylists.html

5. ZD Net, How Stitch Fix uses machine learning to master the science of styling: https://www.zdnet.com/article/how-stitch-fix-uses-machine-learning-to-master-the-science-of-styling/

19
UNILEVER

Using Artificial Intelligence To Streamline Recruiting And Onboarding

International consumer goods manufacturer Unilever sells over 400 branded products in 190 countries. Worldwide, it has over 160,000[1] people, making it one of the world's largest employers.

With any company, people are the most valuable resource. To make sure they are enticing the right talent, Unilever deploys artificial intelligence (AI) solutions aimed at attracting, analyzing and ultimately selecting the best people to fit the thousands of roles it needs to fill each year.

What Problem Is Artificial Intelligence Helping To Solve?

Any recruiting process involves risk. Advertising for talent, screening applicants and onboarding new hires is an expensive and time-consuming process. It has to be done properly though, as hiring the wrong people can have expensive consequences and a damaging impact on business.

Recruiters have limited time available to them to search for the right candidates and once they've come up with a shortlist there is a narrow window of opportunity to make a decision on whether they are a good fit for the role.

In Unilever's case, when recruiting for their Future Leadership program, the company knew it had between four and six months to reduce a pool of 250,000 applicants from all around the word to fill 800 available positions.[2]

The costs don't end once the right person has been found for the job – according to the Society for Human Resource Management, the cost of training a new hire averages out at between six and nine months' wages for the post in question.[3]

How Is Artificial Intelligence Used In Practice?

Unilever partnered with AI recruitment specialists to roll out a global initiative aimed at efficiently matching applicants to posts.

It involved developing a multistage process, which starts with asking applicants from anywhere in the world to submit an online CV or LinkedIn profile.

From there, applicants are asked to take part in 12 different online games. Developed by Pymetrics, the games are designed to test aptitude in a number of different areas relevant to the roles they are applying for.[4]

The games are not necessarily designed to be "won" or "lost" but rather to provide a measure of a candidate's characteristics, and ideal outcomes may be different depending on the role the candidate is applying for.

For example, one game involves inflating balloons to assess a candidate's appetite for risk, using a "stick" or "twist" gameplay mechanic similar to blackjack. Candidates are awarded points for pumping more air into virtual balloons, and must try to stop pumping before the balloon bursts.

The next stage of the process involves submitting a video interview.

As with the games, this can be completed in the candidates' own time using just their smartphones or a computer equipped with a webcam.

Here, AI algorithms analyze the language, facial expressions and body language to determine whether they are likely to fit the profile of someone who will be successful in the role.

From this, a final shortlist of 3,500 applicants was pulled together, who were all invited to assessment centers where they met Unilever recruiters in person for the first time, and the final selection of 800 was made.

Once hired, Unilever's new recruits have access to Unabot, an AI-powered chatbot designed to speed up the onboarding process by answering questions through a natural language chat interface.

What Technology, Tools And Data Were Used?

Pymetric's games allow detailed aptitude profiles to be built up, evaluating candidates' strengths and weaknesses in a more quantitative way than a traditional face-to-face job interview process.

These profiles can then be measured against values that the machine learning algorithms pick out as being likely to signify suitable applicants.

Unilever then uses facial image analytics technology developed by HireVue to interpret the data collected through its pre-recorded video interview process.

Computer vision and natural language processing technology are used to analyze the videos to capture data points that can be autonomously labelled to give readings indicative of characteristics such as "sense of purpose", "systemic thinking", "resilience" or "business acumen".

These characteristics can be matched against those of other people who have proven themselves to be successful in the specific roles being recruited.

Natural language processing also powers Unabot, which is built on Microsoft's Bot Framework.

Using company data from internal documents and company handbooks, it can process questions asked in natural human language and provide answers about the employee's role, company procedures, benefits such as pension plans and even timetables for shuttle buses to and from Unilever's campuses.

What Were The Results?

With 1.8 million applications for employment to process every year, Unilever's Chief HR Officer, Leena Nair, told me that the employee screening process had saved around 70,000 man hours of interviewing time.

As the system also generates automated feedback for applicants, even those who are unsuccessful benefit, she says.

"What I like about the process is that each and every person who applies to us gets some feedback.

"Normally when people send an application to a large company it can go into a 'black hole' – thank you very much for your CV, we'll get back to you – and you never hear from them again.

"All of our applicants get a couple of pages of feedback, how they did in the game, how they did in the video interviews, what characteristics they have that fit, and if they don't fit, the reason why they didn't, and what we think they should do to be successful in a future application.

"It's an example of artificial intelligence allowing us to be more human."

Unabot is being incrementally rolled out across Unilever's global operations. Currently, it is active in 36 of the 190 countries where Unilever operates.

Nair tells me that 36% of staff have engaged with it so far, and 80% of those who do go on to become repeat users.

Users asked to rate how satisfied they are with the answers it provides currently, rate the system at 3.9 out of a maximum score of 5.

Key Challenges, Learning Points And Takeaways

- Having the capability to assess applications from hundreds of thousands of people means more applicants can be considered for a role.

- It also means that those who are likely to be successful are less likely to slip through the net than when the process depends on a human recruiter sifting through piles of CVs.

- Human recruiters would not have the time to carry out this initial screening and analysis manually, but AI and machine learning mean that a shortlist can be quickly drawn up, no matter how many initial applications are made.

- Chatbots provide hassle-free interfaces where employees and new hires can quickly get answers to common questions, and AI is used to understand which answers people are most likely to need.

Notes

1. Unilever: https://www.unilever.com/about/who-we-are/about-Unilever/
2. Hirevue, Unilever finds top talent faster with Hirevue assessments: https://www.hirevue.com/customers/global-talent-acquisition-unilever-case-study
3. Huffington Post, High Turnover Costs Way More Than You Think: https://www.huffingtonpost.com/julie-kantor/high-turnover-costs-way-more-than-you-think_b_9197238.html
4. Business Insider, Consumer-goods giant Unilever has been hiring employees using brain games and artificial intelligence – and it's a huge success: http://uk.businessinsider.com/unilever-artificial-intelligence-hiring-process-2017-6

20
WALMART

Using Artificial Intelligence To Keep Shelves Stacked And Customers Happy

With over 11,000 retail stores worldwide, Walmart is the world's biggest company by revenue[1] as well as the largest private employer with around 2.3 million employees. Its online and offline retailing operations are deeply interlinked as part of the company's strategy – real-world stores double as warehouses for its e-commerce business,[2] while artificial intelligence (AI) and big data initiatives initially developed for e-commerce are also put to work on the shop floor.

From pioneering customer data gathering through loyalty schemes to its latest robotic, artificially intelligent shelf-scanning robots, Walmart has ensured it has kept itself at the technological cutting edge for decades.

What Problem Is Artificial Intelligence Helping To Solve?

With so many stores, tracking inventory is a major challenge for enterprises of Walmart's scale. To remain competitive in a market where businesses sink or swim on price and customer convenience, it must consistently and accurately predict customer buying trends, where locality, weather patterns, customer demographics and economic conditions all have an impact.

Without very close to real-time sensing, accurately monitoring how products are shipped and sold is challenging. Often it will involve different inventory systems being used by different departments. Siloed data may not be available at the moment its needed, and the data itself is subject to human error due to being manually collected or updated.

A customer-centric example would be in-store apps that let shoppers locate particular items on a supermarket's shelves. These have existed for a while and, as anyone who's tried one will know, can be hit and miss. This is because many things can happen between items being stacked onto shelves and the next time it will be "sensed" – as it is beeped through the checkout – which could render the data uploaded to the app outdated.

How Is Artificial Intelligence Used In Practice?

The fine line that all big retailers tread is between keeping prices down and offering conveniences to their customers. The slightest wobble along this path can lead to losing market share to competitors.

In one particularly interesting initiative, autonomous, shelf-scanning robots have been deployed to bring real-time video analytics to the shop floor.

These robots, installed in a trial capacity initially in a small number of US stores, patrol the aisles capturing video footage of products on the shelves. This means that Walmart's data on how stock levels on the shop floor fluctuate hour to hour between replenishments is virtually real time.

As a result, more accurate models of customer behavior can be built with better predictions of what items will sell at different times of the day. This data is of course fed back to supply chain and inventory systems, which will more accurately forecast demand.

In the example given above of the customer in-store app, real-time data relayed from the robot's sensors can tell app users exactly where items are on the shelves – rather than where they should be, according to a separate database.

Crucially, at a time when the long-term impacts of automation on human workforces is starting to be considered, Walmart robots are not intended to replace humans.[3] Rather, they are designed specifically to assist with very routine (boring) manual tasks. This will free up shop floor staff to spend time assisting customers.

What Technology, Tools And Data Were Used

Walmart's robots are designed by California, US-based Bossa Nova Robotics.[4] They stand around two feet in height and are equipped with extendable cameras and sensors for scanning higher shelves.

Bossa Nova recently announced that the capabilities of its robots – including those used by Walmart – are set to be enhanced thanks to the acquisition of Hawxeye, which specializes in computer vision technology. Hawxeye's technology is notable because it carries out machine learning directly on a device – such as a camera – rather than first having to send data to the cloud.[5] This increases speed and reduces the amount of data of no value, which has to be stored and processed by server-side systems.

The robots operate in the same manner as autonomous vehicles, and are able to recognize obstacles (such as people) in their path in real time and avoid colliding with them. They do this using cameras, which monitor their immediate surroundings.

Walmart's robots are designed to operate while stores are open by applying machine learning algorithms to safely go about their business in busy, public environments.[6]

In 2017, Walmart said it was working on the construction of the world's biggest private cloud, capable of processing 2.5 petabytes of data every hour.[7] It contains e-commerce and in-store transactional data, CRM records, customer feedback, social media and bought-in third party data. Data collected by the in-store robots will undoubtedly feed into this too, to help make stocking decisions around the world.

Their analytics platform is built on largely open source technologies, which gives data science teams the flexibility of picking between industry standard software solutions without having to code them themselves or buy expensive, closed proprietary solutions from third parties.

For its inventory and supply chain processes it uses tools, including Apache Spark, Cassandra and Kafka.[8] These data tools are geared towards enabling real-time analysis of very large, fast-changing datasets. Insights from the data are visualized in Tableau, meaning they can be quickly understood by the humans who need to act on them.

What Were The Results?

Initial tests of the shelf-scanning robots were successful enough to warrant rolling the pilot out to a total of 50 US stores.

Customers benefit from the added convenience that there is a higher likelihood the product will be stocked and on the right shelf for them to find when they need it. Walmart benefits by reducing wasted expenditure and shelf space on items that aren't going to sell.

Bossa Nova's chief business officer, Martin Hitch, told *Forbes:* "We already know with an incredibly high degree of accuracy what gets shipped into the store and what gets sold through the register. Now, for the first time, we also know that we're selling so many products because we have the right number of them on display at certain points in the day."[9]

Key Challenges, Learning Points And Takeaways

- When you're Walmart and your competitors are the likes of Amazon and Alibaba, AI isn't a choice today – it's a basic necessity for survival.

- Big retailers tread the path between minimizing costs and maximizing customer convenience. If AI and data initiatives are well planned and executed, they can sometimes do both.

- In businesses of Walmart's scale, dependent on a highly complex network of moving parts, many small efficiencies can add up to major gains.

- Walmart says its robots are not designed to replace human workers, and it may very well be making that statement in good faith today. But the long-term implications of automating large numbers of functions typically carried out by humans are still largely unknown.

Notes

1. Walmart, Walmart 2018 Annual Report: http://s2.q4cdn.com/056532643/files/doc_financials/2018/annual/WMT-2018_Annual-Report.pdf
2. Fortune, Five Moves Walmart is Making to Compete with Amazon and Target: http://fortune.com/2017/09/27/5-moves-walmart-is-making-to-compete-with-amazon-and-target/
3. Business Insider, Walmart reveals why it has robots roaming the aisles in 50 of its stores: http://uk.businessinsider.com/walmart-robots-in-50-stores-2018-3
4. The Verge, Walmart is using shelf-scanning robots to audit its stores: https://www.theverge.com/2017/10/27/16556864/walmart-introduces-shelf-scanning-robots

5. Venturebeat, Bossa Nova Robotics acquires Hawxeye to improve inventory object detection: https://venturebeat.com/2018/07/18/bossa-nova-robotics-acquires-hawxeye-to-improve-inventory-object-detection/
6. Crunchbase: https://www.crunchbase.com/organization/bossa-nova-robotics-inc#section-overview
7. Forbes, Really Big Data At Walmart: Real-Time Insights From Their 40+ Petabyte Data Cloud: https://www.forbes.com/sites/bernardmarr/2017/01/23/really-big-data-at-walmart-real-time-insights-from-their-40-petabyte-data-cloud/#2a7bee6b6c10
8. WalmartLabs, How we build a robust analytics platform using Spark, Kafka and Cassandra: https://medium.com/walmartlabs/how-we-build-a-robust-analytics-platform-using-spark-kafka-and-cassandra-lambda-architecture-70c2d1bc8981
9. Forbes, This Shelf-Scanning Robot Could Be Coming To A Store Near You: https://www.forbes.com/sites/jenniferjohnson/2018/06/29/this-shelf-scanning-robot-could-be-coming-to-a-store-near-you/#b0a32c73fb1c

Part 3
MEDIA, ENTERTAINMENT AND TELECOM COMPANIES

21
THE WALT DISNEY COMPANY

Using Artificial Intelligence To Make Magical Memories

Disney's Magic Kingdom theme park sells itself as "the most magical place on Earth". Since the first park opened in California in 1955, technology has played a part in bringing that magic to life.

With more than 56,000 guests arriving on the average day, each expecting a magical experience, park planners and entertainers (called "cast members") have the task of making sure everyone goes home with only good memories.

Queues, congestion and overbooked attractions certainly aren't magical. So, The Walt Disney Company has turned towards advanced data analytics and smart technology to remove the "friction" from their theme parks.

What Problem Is Artificial Intelligence Used To Solve?

With tens of thousands of visitors each wanting to experience as many of the hundreds of attractions in each park as they possibly can on any given day, coordinating the flow of humans is a highly complex operation.

The headline attractions – the newest and hottest rides, as well as the legendary favorites – create bottlenecks. It's frustrating for the visitors if they feel they are standing around all day, and when they're in line, they aren't spending money at the ice cream stands and gift shops. Which is frustrating for Walt Disney.

On top of that, those ice cream stands, as well as hundreds of other food and drink outlets, have to be kept stocked with refreshments and optimally located to catch passing trade at the right moment.

How Is Artificial Intelligence Used In Practice?

In 2013, Disney introduced its MagicBand wristbands, which are issued to every visitor and let them book rides and attractions, access their hotel rooms, order meals at the park's restaurants and pay for purchases in gift shops.

They also give Disney detailed information about what each visitor is doing at every point in the day. This lets them offer personalized experiences – for example, allowing restaurant staff to greet them by their names when they arrive. It also gives park planners detailed aggregated datasets about overall visitor movements.

This means that planners can repurpose spots that fail to attract footfall to ease congestion around the top attractions and hotspots that cause bottlenecks throughout the day.

Because data is analyzed in real time, response can be real time too – for example, staging an impromptu character parade to draw crowds from a heavily congested area to a quieter one.[1]

The bands are part of a wider Disney initiative called MyMagic+, which involves removing "friction" – unnecessary stress – from visitors at every point of their Disney journey, starting from when they book their tickets online.

The system lets visitors use the My Disney Experience app to plan what attractions they want to visit, where they want to eat and which characters they want to meet. It then presents them with an automated schedule designed to minimize crowds and waiting, while doing everything on the visitor's list.

Hotel visitors don't even need to check in – the wrist band automatically tells the hotel staff that the guests have arrived, and families can head straight to their room and use the band to unlock the door.

It's also worth noting that the wider Walt Disney Company is active in artificial intelligence (AI) and machine learning research through its Disney Research initiative.[2]

The facilities allow the company to partner with universities on initiatives involving AI, visual computing and robotics. Their academic links give them the opportunity to develop technology solutions that could be used across the Disney empire. Innovations originating in the labs have applications in Disney theme parks, films, video games and television shows.

One recent breakthrough has been the development of a system for speeding up the rendering of graphics in its Pixar computer-generated movies. It involves using deep learning convolutional neural networks to eliminate "noise" generated during the rendering of the 3D graphics. This means that each frame can be rendered at a lower fidelity and still result in a production-quality image.[3]

Disney is also working on a tool to measure real-time audience reactions in its motion theatres.[4] Here, it uses deep learning algorithms that have been trained to watch an audience of hundreds of people in a darkened theatre to analyze their facial expressions to determine if they are, for example, happy, sad, bored, etc. This gives Disney real-time insights into audience engagement and could potentially be a move towards responsive experiences that change according to what people enjoy or how they react.

What Technology, Tools And Data Are Used?

Like any good magician, Disney is notoriously secretive about the technology at work behind the scenes, which is used to create the magic!

However, it is known that Disney's MagicBand wristbands use radio-frequency identification technology to communicate with thousands of sensors positioned around its parks. They also contain a radio device similar to those used in mobile phones for longer range communication.[5]

Rolling out the initiative cost around $1 billion and required Disney to integrate every facet of the park that visitors interact with – turnstiles, hotel room doors, rides and point-of-purchase terminals – into its data capture systems.[6]

This means that data points are created whenever guests use the wristband to check into rides, restaurants or shows, order food or make purchases at gift shops.

While it was being designed, the team responsible built a large-scale "demo" of the system on a disused soundstage at the theme park. Individual rooms were built and decorated to represent each stage of the customer journey, such as a living room to represent the point where the customers first book their holiday online, and a mini replica of the Haunted Mansion attraction, to represent a park attraction.[7]

This was essential as it helped the theme park staff and management, who weren't used to large-scale technological disruption of their working processes, to buy into the concept.

Disney worked with outside partners, including Accenture, HP and Synapse, on the MyMagic+ program.

What Were The Results?

Visitors to the Magic Kingdom can cram a lot more into their day and go home with better memories (and more souvenirs and merchandise) if the "friction" can be removed from their trip. Less waiting in line leads to happier customers who are more likely to return.

Disney says that uptake of the services offered through MyMagic+ and MagicBands has been high, with 80% of visitors using the technology to make reservations for their rides.[8]

Key Challenges, Learning Points And Takeaways

- Disney uses its theme parks to bring its characters and movies into its visitors' real lives. It hopes this will make them bond more closely with its brands and franchises, and continue to buy its movies and tie-in merchandise.

- This is more likely to happen if they have a good experience during their visit – advanced, intelligent analytics can vastly simplify managing the movement of huge numbers of people.

- Among the many arms of the Disney corporation, the parks division was known for being risk averse with new technology.[9] Overcoming this was a challenge for the team that built the MyMagic+ initiative.

Notes

1. Fast Company, The Messy Business Of Reinventing Happiness: https://www.fastcompany.com/3044283/the-messy-business-of-reinventing-happiness#chapter-Discovery_Island
2. Disney Research: https://www.disneyresearch.com/
3. Disney Research: https://www.disneyresearch.com/innovations/denoising/
4. CNBC, Watching you, watching it: Disney turns to AI to track filmgoers' true feelings about its films: https://www.cbc.ca/news/technology/disney-ai-real-time-tracking-fvae-1.4233063
5. Wired, Disney's $1 Billion Bet on a Magic Wristband: https://www.wired.com/2015/03/disney-magicband/
6. USA Today, Disney parks tech upgrades make visiting more convenient: https://eu.usatoday.com/story/travel/experience/america/themeparks/2018/02/27/disney-parks-magicbands-fastpasses-app/374588002/
7. Fast Company, The Messy Business Of Reinventing Happiness: https://www.fastcompany.com/3044283/the-messy-business-of-reinventing-happiness
8. USA Today, Disney parks tech upgrades make visiting more convenient: https://eu.usatoday.com/story/travel/experience/america/themeparks/2018/02/27/disney-parks-magicbands-fastpasses-app/374588002/
9. Fast Company, The Messy Business Of Reinventing Happiness: https://www.fastcompany.com/3044283/the-messy-business-of-reinventing-happiness#chapter-Discovery_Island

22
INSTAGRAM

*Using Artificial Intelligence To Tackle
Online Bullying*

Instagram has only been around since 2010 but already there's a generation that probably can't imagine life without it.

The Facebook-owned social network, which focuses on image and video sharing, has 1 billion active users as of June 2018,[1] posting 95 million pictures every day.[2]

Recognizing that bullying, harassment and abuse are unfortunately frequent occurrences online, Instagram has announced that it is rolling out artificial intelligence (AI) to stop unpleasant behavior in its tracks before it affects people's lives.

What Problems Is Artificial Intelligence Helping To Solve?

Behind all those sun-kissed holiday selfies and stunning scenery, there's a darker aspect to social image sharing.

UK charity Ditch The Label's annual bullying survey found that 42% of young people had experience of being cyberbullied on Instagram[3] – the highest figure for any social platform.

In its report Cyberbullying's Impact on Young People's Mental Health, the Children's Society found early in 2018 that "the steps being taken by social media companies in response to cyberbullying are inadequate and inconsistent".[4]

Like real bullying, cyberbullying can have a deep and lasting impact on its victims' lives, in extreme cases leading to mental health issues and suicide.

By taking responsibility for keeping their users safe from bullying and harassment, social media companies have to walk a tightrope between restricting freedom of speech and policing users' content.

How Is Artificial Intelligence Used In Practice?

Instagram rolled out artificially intelligent comment filtering algorithms, which screen all comments uploaded to the network.[5]

The filter is switched on by default on all accounts, but can be deactivated if someone really feels they need an uncensored experience.

Text, as well as speech in videos, is parsed by the filter, and anything that is determined to be an abusive comment – insults about someone's appearance, or their race or gender, for example – is automatically filtered.

When particular accounts are highlighted as being frequently filtered, it will trigger a manual review from the network's human staff, who will determine if the user behind the account is breaching its terms of service. This could lead to them being barred from using the platform.

What Technology, Tools And Data Are Used?

Instagram's anti-bullying filter uses natural language processing technology called DeepText, which was developed by Facebook.

It works by examining the text that makes up users' comments and working out if they show patterns that fit with other uploads that have been flagged for abuse.

DeepText uses deep learning involving neural networks to classify the text used in uploads, as well as the context set by the text. Because deep learning systems improve in accuracy as they are trained, it becomes increasingly able to distinguish, for example, insults thrown between friends in jest and language that is indicative of a targeted campaign of cyber-harassment.[6]

In common with other natural language-based deep learning systems, it is able to learn and adapt to the way humans communicate in text to become increasingly good at understanding slang, patterns of speech, regional language variations and turns-of-phrase.

Where Facebook says that it is breaking new ground with DeepText is in additional layers of meaning it assigns to each word as it carries out its analytics.

As well as assigning an identifying tag to each word, and using it to track a word's frequency and context in a piece of text, it assigns each word a position on a web of semantic connections.

These allow the AI to learn about common relationships between words, and situations where different words are used to mean the same thing.

The trick is that it can do this so fast that the system is effective in real time. Which means analyzing, understanding and making a decision about 1,000 Instagram uploads per second.

What Were The Results?

Instagram's anti-bullying initiative is very new and the company hasn't spoken about the results it has seen yet.

However, the hope is that by removing offensive, upsetting or hurtful comments before they can be seen, users will have a more positive and inclusive experience on the platform.

Key Challenges, Learning Points And Takeaways

- Bullying is a problem that's always existed in society, but the internet and social media make matters worse as victims can be targeted publicly and anonymously.

- Without AI it wasn't possible to screen every upload to Instagram in real time. This meant that proactive blocking as enabled by DeepText wouldn't be possible.

- There's also less risk of inadvertently infringing on someone simply exercising free speech or their right to object or disagree. Text analytics and natural language processing are advanced enough now to reliably make the right call.

Notes

1. Statista, Number of monthly active Instagram users from January 2013 to June 2018 (in millions): https://www.statista.com/statistics/253577/number-of-monthly-active-instagram-users/
2. Sprout Social, 18 Instagram Stats Every Marketer Should Know for 2018: https://sproutsocial.com/insights/instagram-stats/
3. Ditch The Label, Anti-Bullying Survey 2017: https://www.ditchthelabel.org/wp-content/uploads/2017/07/The-Annual-Bullying-Survey-2017-1.pdf
4. The Children's Society, Cyberbullying's Impact on Young People's Mental Health: https://www.childrenssociety.org.uk/sites/default/files/social-media-cyberbullying-inquiry-summary-report.pdf

5. Instagram, Protecting Our Community from Bullying Comments: https://instagram-press.com/blog/2018/05/01/protecting-our-community-from-bullying-comments-2/
6. Facebook, Introducing DeepText: Facebook's text understanding engine: https://code.fb.com/core-data/introducing-deeptext-facebook-s-text-understanding-engine/

23
LINKEDIN

Using Artificial Intelligence To Solve The Skills Crisis

LinkedIn has built a social network for the professional world. What Facebook has done for keeping us in touch with friends and family, LinkedIn replicates for our working lives.

So, while Facebook primarily makes its money selling our data to businesses so they can advertise products to us, LinkedIn's revenue comes from employers looking to entice us to join their ranks.

Instead of categorizing us by what movies or music we click "like" on, it looks at our job skills and experience. Then it uses artificial intelligence (AI), which is baked into every feature on its platform, to match us with opportunities or bring us to the attention of prospective employers.

What Problem Is Artificial Intelligence Helping To Solve?

Matching applicants to job roles is a challenging and expensive task for businesses – according to Glassdoor, the average hire in the United States costs a company $4,000.[1]

That's a fair chunk of money even if you get lucky and find someone good – however, evidence seems to suggest humans aren't particularly great at selecting the right person for the job.

A study last year by the UK Recruitment and Employment Confederation found that businesses were failing to make the right hires for two out of every five roles.[2] It also calculates that an unsuccessful hire at middle management level can cost a company an average of £132,000.

Part of this inefficiency is that recruiters have traditionally been able to gather little information during the recruitment process. Often all they have to go on will be a person's CV, interview performance and references.

In addition, particular professions are challenging to recruit for – whether it's due to lack of skills or lack of willing applicants within a geographic area. Teaching is one example where 100,000 US classrooms began the 2016/17 academic year with a teacher not qualified to teach.[3]

Meanwhile, according to the American Association of Colleges of Nursing, over 1 million more nurses will need to be recruited by 2024 to cope with the ageing population.[4]

Technology in particular faces a skills crisis. The AI revolution itself, which is sometimes predicted to cause widespread human unemployment, is actually having the opposite effect at the moment.

The rush by industry to embrace AI, coupled with the difficulty in finding candidates, means there will be 2.7 million unfilled vacancies in data science by 2020, according to IBM.[5]

Inefficiencies in finding candidates to fill any of these vacancies could have ruinous consequences beyond each respective industry, with knock-on effects impacting the entire economy.

How Is Artificial Intelligence Used In Practice?

LinkedIn gathers data on millions of professionals and then uses AI search tools to match applicants with jobs, and vice versa.

It also lets us build our network by suggesting people we know and might like to connect with, and uses AI analytics to identify these connections.

It even uses AI to suggest courses you could benefit from, from its library of LinkedIn learning courses.

Those looking for work have the option to mark themselves as "open candidates", meaning they have indicated they are open to new opportunities.

LinkedIn assesses information the user has given as well as details about how they use their profile – what jobs they browse, for example – to build up a profile.[6]

When an employer indicates that they are looking for candidates, LinkedIn's algorithms match them with candidates who fit the profile of others who have successfully filled similar vacancies.

As the system uses machine learning, it is continuously refining its algorithms based on feedback from previous matches.

This means it can become increasingly good at predicting who will be the best candidate to fill a role. Its criteria for making the selection may be something that would go entirely unnoticed by a human recruiter with a pile of CVs to sift through.

But machine learning will build patterns in the links between the types of candidates who successfully fill different vacancies, with increasing confidence in its predictions.

LinkedIn also says that AI is a part of the process it uses to design its services. This means data-driven insights are used to determine what features and functionality users will get from the platform in the future.

What Technology, Tools And Data Were Used?

LinkedIn uses data that users give the social media account about their professional lives, such as their work experience, skills, achievements and where they are willing to relocate to.

It uses this to build a picture of which vacancies might tempt them to reply, and categorize them according to the probability that they will respond to enquires or fit a particular role.

It also builds up profiles as they use the service by monitoring what companies and vacancies they browse, as well as who joins their personal network.

LinkedIn's Recruiter platform, which businesses use to find candidates for their vacancies, also collects data on its users' search and browsing activities.

This data is used to profile recruiters and tries to build models that predict what they're looking for in recruits.[7]

What Were The Results?

LinkedIn say that improvements to the AI algorithms used in its tools and search engines increased the response rate to its users' InMail messages by 45%, and the number of conversations started between recruiters and candidates doubled, in one year.[8]

The social network has also announced that all of its software engineers will be trained to use AI, particularly deep learning, due to confidence that it can bring improvements to any aspect of its business where it is deployed.[9]

Key Challenges, Learning Points And Takeaways

- Like any social network, LinkedIn's fuel is the data its users feed it, and what it can learn from their behavior as they use its services.

- Machine learning algorithms can be used to accurately match candidates with job vacancies, but they need the data to be able to do it.

- AI job matching can encourage employers to consider candidates with experience and skillsets that differ from their preconceptions about what a job requires.

Notes

1. Glassdoor, How To Calculate Cost-Per-Hire: https://www.glassdoor.com/employers/blog/calculate-cost-per-hire/
2. The Recruitment and Employment Confederation, Hiring mistakes are costing UK businesses billions each year – REC: https://www.rec.uk.com/news-and-policy/press-releases/hiring-mistakes-are-costing-uk-businesses-billions-each-year-rec
3. The Week, America's Teaching Shortage: http://theweek.com/articles/797112/americas-teacher-shortage
4. American Association of Colleges of Nursing, Nursing Shortage Fact Sheet: https://www.aacnnursing.org/News-Information/Fact-Sheets/Nursing-Shortage
5. IBM, The Quant Crunch: https://www.01.ibm.com/common/ssi/cgi-bin/ssialias?htmlfid=IML14576USEN&

6. LinkedIn, How LinkedIn Uses Automation and AI to Power Recruiting Tools: https://business.linkedin.com/talent-solutions/blog/product-updates/2017/how-linkedin-uses-automation-and-ai-to-power-recruiting-tools

7. LinkedIn, How LinkedIn Uses Automation and AI to Power Recruiting Tools: https://business.linkedin.com/talent-solutions/blog/product-updates/2017/how-linkedin-uses-automation-and-ai-to-power-recruiting-tools

8. LinkedIn, How LinkedIn Uses Automation and AI to Power Recruiting Tools: https://business.linkedin.com/talent-solutions/blog/product-updates/2017/how-linkedin-uses-automation-and-ai-to-power-recruiting-tools

9. VentureBeat, LinkedIn plans to teach all its engineers the basics of using AI: https://venturebeat.com/2017/10/24/linkedin-plans-to-teach-all-its-engineers-the-basics-of-using-ai/

24
NETFLIX

Using Artificial Intelligence To Give Us A Better TV Experience

Netflix evolved from a DVD-by-mail rental company to become a subscription-based streaming video-on-demand service with 130 million subscribers worldwide.[1]

Netflix doesn't (yet) show advertising on its platform, but generates revenue from the subscription fees its customers pay. The driving force behind its sustainability is that customers feel they are getting good value for money for their monthly fee.

To ensure this, Netflix's TV and movie output is geared towards the concept of "binge watching" – essentially keeping customers glued to their TV sets for extended periods of time. The theory (which seems to be working out) being that this will make them feel their subscription fee is a worthwhile investment.

What Problem Is Artificial Intelligence Helping To Solve?

Consumers aren't exactly short of entertainment options these days. Between streaming movie services, the internet, video games and traditional broadcast TV, there are thousands of channels and services vying for our attention as we sit glued to our sofas during down-time.

In the "old days", scheduling was seen as a precise science, and TV networks carefully selected what programs would run at what times to fit in with our lives and earn our loyalty.

For example, scheduling news bulletins in the early evening when we return from work, followed by light entertainment as we relax in the evenings and a late-night movie before bedtime.

With on-demand forms of entertainment, this is often no longer possible. Customers being able to watch what they want, when they want, caused a quandary. What if they consistently pick the wrong programs to watch, and end up not feeling they are getting sufficient entertainment bang for their buck?

How Is Artificial Intelligence Used In Practice?

Netflix uses artificial intelligence (AI) to predict which of its catalog of more than 10,000 movies and TV shows you are likely to want to watch next.

These are the recommendations that pop up immediately after a movie or show finishes, as well as the content that appears in the service's menus when Netflix loads up on your TV, laptop or tablet.

Netflix originally used IMDB ratings together with the user's past viewing habits, and indications they give about shows they are interested in when they first sign up, to come up with a "personalized schedule" of content that it thinks a viewer will be interested in.[2]

Since then, Netflix has built up a huge dataset of viewing habits – on 7 January 2018 alone, its viewers set a record by streaming 350 million hours of content in one day.[3]

This means it knows an awful lot about what shows and movies people with similar habits to yourself are likely to enjoy.

What Technology, Tools And Data Were Used?

The most significant data that goes into its personalized scheduling algorithms is individual customers' past viewing habits.

Netflix developed (and open sourced) its own deep learning library called Vectorflow to process the data it collects on customer viewing.[4]

Essentially, this is a recommendation engine – a key use case for AI technology as used by Amazon for product recommendations and Facebook with its "people you may know" features.

Netflix breaks down its content (movies and shows) and tags them according to individual elements – action films, psychological thrillers, female protagonists – there are tens of thousands of different tags that can be assigned to individual pieces of content.

It then measures how content that fits these tags matches with individuals' viewing preferences. When it finds that particular tags work well with viewers that match a particular profile (based on their viewing history), it will recommend that content to others who also match that profile.

It is also used for a number of other functions across the service, such as optimizing streaming quality to ensure users receive the best possible picture quality.

When Netflix data scientists develop new machine learning methods that potentially provide more accurate predictions about what their customers will want to watch, they test them by initially rolling them out to a subset of customers.

If they find that the overall metrics improve, then it will be rolled out across the network. These metrics include the number of hours of content watched by the customers, as well as the churn rate – the rate at which customers cancel their subscriptions because they can't find anything to watch.[5]

To optimize the streaming and picture quality, Netflix uses algorithms that analyze every frame in real time to work out how it can be compressed to the smallest size possible, while still retaining all of the data that makes up the image people will see.[6]

Elements of each frame such as lighting, complexity (how individual parts of the image differ from others) and how much of the image will be moving in the next frame are all considered by the algorithm.

What Were The Results?

Netflix is able to accurately recommend content to viewers based on their preferences, and the preferences of others who match their profile. This leads to customers who re-subscribe for longer, offering longer lifetime value to the company.

As a content producer itself, it is also able to create new movies and TV shows that more closely match what its viewers want to watch.

Netflix's AI compression algorithms for minimizing the size of files that have to be transmitted, and therefore improving streaming quality, managed to reduce data usage by a factor of 1,000.

An episode of *Jessica Jones*, which would otherwise require 750 megabits per second of bandwidth, was reduced to 750 kilobits.[7]

Key Challenges, Learning Points And Takeaways

- Moving from a mail-order to a subscription model vastly increased the amount of data that Netflix was able to collect, not just about what customers watch, but how and when they watch it.

- Providing customers with more accurate recommendations about what they might want to watch means that fewer customers will cancel their subscriptions due to not being able to find movies and shows they will enjoy.

- AI enables these recommendations to become finely tuned, as they learn from an ever-growing dataset of customer habits.

- Netflix was able to use the vast database of viewing habits it built up to begin producing its own output, guided by data on what its customers want.

- Streaming high definition and ultra-high definition video uses huge bandwidth resources – resources that are limited and expensive. AI can reduce these overheads by learning to transmit only the important data.

Notes

1. Netflix, Shareholder's letter, 16 July 16 2018: https://s22.q4cdn.com/959853165/files/doc_financials/quarterly_reports/2018/q2/FINAL-Q2-18-Shareholder-Letter.pdf
2. It's Foss, Netflix Open Source AI: https://itsfoss.com/netflix-open-source-ai/
3. Variety, Netflix Subscribers Streamed Record-Breaking 350 Million Hours of Video on Jan. 7: https://variety.com/2018/digital/news/netflix-350-million-hours-1202721679
4. Netflix, Introducing Vectorflow: https://medium.com/@NetflixTechBlog/introducing-vectorflow-fe10d7f126b8

5. Nvidia, How Netflix Uses AI: https://blogs.nvidia.com/blog/2018/06/01/how-netflix-uses-ai/
6. The Motley Fool, Netflix Streaming gets an AI Upgrade: https://www.fool.com/investing/2018/03/15/netflix-streaming-gets-an-ai-upgrade.aspx
7. The Motley Fool, Netflix Streaming gets an AI Upgrade: https://www.fool.com/investing/2018/03/15/netflix-streaming-gets-an-ai-upgrade.aspx

25
PRESS ASSOCIATION

Using Artificial Intelligence To Cover Local News Stories

The Press Association (commonly referred to as PA) is a UK-based news agency that provides text and video news stories, photography, copywriting, TV listings and sports coverage to local, regional and national newspapers, magazines and TV stations across the country.

In 2017, it announced a partnership with Urbs Media to roll out news stories written by artificial intelligence (AI) "journalists" to local newspapers.

What Problems Is Artificial Intelligence Helping To Solve?

The local news industry in the United Kingdom has been in decline since the arrival of the internet, with more people turning to social media and online sites to keep up with local events. This has led to newspapers closing and journalists being made redundant.[1]

This has left a gap that has been described as "dangerous for democracy". Local newspapers in effect operated as the "eyes and ears" of the general public into local political matters and regional administration, as well as matters involving healthcare and criminal justice.

Without reporters covering these beats, the public can't hold local authorities to account, and demand answers when they are needed.

How Is Artificial Intelligence Used In Practice?

PA partnered with data-driven journalism specialists Urbs Media to build an AI system capable of mass-producing localized news stories based on data that is fed into it.

While still employing human journalists to pinpoint the stories that are in need of coverage, the system uses AI algorithms to tell the story, and localizes it for newspapers and websites around the country.[2]

The service – known as Reporters and Data and Robots (RADAR) – was funded through a grant from Google's Digital News Initiative Fund, which aims to help journalism thrive in the digital age by harnessing new advances in technology.[3]

RADAR says that the project is not supposed to replace human journalists, but will make it easier for them to cover stories in a way that is relevant to local audiences by spotting trends in datasets such as government open data.

It then creates localized news reports explaining the impact of these trends at a local level.

As well as established local newspapers and outlets, the stories are available to the new breed of "hyperlocal" news sites that have sprung up in many communities to fill the gap left by the declining local newspaper industry.[4]

What Technology, Tools And Data Were Used?

The key AI technology used in the RADAR project is natural language processing and generation.[5]

This means it can "read" tables of statistics and information and parse them into news stories in human, natural language (English in this case).

For example, if it is given a list of average wait times that occur when members of the public call for an ambulance, it will be able to localize these by inferring which regions have good response times, average response times or poor response times.

Most of the data used is taken from open datasets published by government agencies, covering areas such as healthcare, education, law and order or demographic data.

What Are The Results?

News stories created with the RADAR system are now available to more than 1,000 local news outlets through the PA news feed.[6]

Mass-scale localization of news stories means there is more chance that important issues will be brought to the public's attention via local news outlets whose budgets are extremely tight.

When the AI surfaces issues that demand more in-depth and rigorous investigation, then human journalists can be assigned to stories to look for issues such as underlying causes that are not obvious from the data.

The stories can also help combat the problem of "fake news" – as it has been shown that when journalists neglect to cover issues of local importance, there is usually someone ready to provide their own take on the matter, and often this will be driven by personal or anecdotal experience rather than hard facts and data.

Overall this should lead to a more informed public, which has the information it needs at its fingertips to make decisions through local democracy.

Key Challenges, Learning Points And Takeaways

- Local news outlets are severely pressured by budget constraints, which has left a potentially dangerous hole in their ability to cover issues of local importance.

- AI can quickly and accurately compile news reports in easy-to-understand natural human language, simply using public datasets.

- This will leave less room in the news ecosphere for peddlers of misinformation and "fake news".

- Human journalists will have more time available to carry out in-depth investigations into the background issues that may not be picked up by the AI working on the data alone.

Notes

1. BBC, Death of the Local Newspaper: https://www.bbc.co.uk/news/uk-43106436

2. The Drum, How PA and Urbs Media will use robots to strengthen local news, rather than devalue it: https://www.thedrum.com/opinion/2017/08/10/how-pa-and-urbs-media-will-use-robots-strengthen-local-news-rather-devalue-it

3. Google, Radar (Round 3): https://newsinitiative.withgoogle.com/dnifund/dni-projects/radar/

4. Press Association, More than 1,000 UK regional news titles now have access to stories jointly written by journalists and AI as RADAR launches new website: https://www.pressassociation.com/2018/06/18/more-than-1000-uk-regional-news-titles-now-have-access-to-stories-jointly-written-by-journalists-and-ai-as-radar-launches-new-website/

5. Press Association, Trial of automated news service underway as RADAR makes its first editorial hires: https://www.pressassociation.com/2017/12/12/trial-automated-news-service-underway-radar-makes-first-editorial-hires/

6. Press Association, More than 1,000 UK regional news titles now have access to stories jointly written by journalists and AI as RADAR launches new website: https://www.pressassociation.com/2018/06/18/more-than-1000-uk-regional-news-titles-now-have-access-to-stories-jointly-written-by-journalists-and-ai-as-radar-launches-new-website/

26
SPOTIFY

Using Artificial Intelligence To Find New Music You Will Love

Spotify is a streaming music service that launched in 2008 and now has 180 million active users and 83 million subscribers.[1]

Like other online services that have risen to prominence in the last decade, such as Amazon and Netflix, offering its users a large catalog of content at prices that undercut traditional delivery methods is only part of the recipe for success.

The "icing on the cake" is Spotify's advanced predictive technology powered by machine learning. This makes it possible to present that content in a way that people can make sense of and enjoy.

One successful way it has managed this is through its Discover Weekly playlists, which give users an artificial intelligence (AI)-curated playlist of new music it thinks they will enjoy.

What Problems Is Artificial Intelligence Helping To Solve?

With millions of songs at their fingertips, users are never short of music to listen to. However, they may find it difficult to discover new bands and artists in the way that radio listeners did in the past.

While it may be simple enough for them to search their favorite band's or singer's name and hear their latest releases, unearthing new talent from the thousands of new tracks added to the service every day is a trickier proposition.

How Is Artificial Intelligence Used In Practice?

Spotify presents users with 30 new tracks every week that it thinks they will love via their own personal Discover Weekly playlist.

To those of us who grew up making mix tapes for our friends by copying songs onto cassette, it's like having a new best friend who happens to be an AI.

Another way to look at it would be to think of the AI as filling a role traditionally played by the radio DJ – reading their audience's taste and playing songs they think they will enjoy.

One breakthrough that led to the Discover Weekly podcast was the realization that it wasn't just what Spotify recommends that matters to users, but also how it recommendeds it.[2]

As users have become used to the "playlist" concept as a form of music curation since the early days of digital music, it made sense that Spotify uses this format for presenting its automated recommendations.

What Technology, Tools And Data Were Used?

As with Netflix's recommendation engines, data for Spotify's Discover Weekly playlists is gathered by monitoring its users' listening habits.

This makes it possible to begin to build up recommendations through a process called collaborative filtering.[3]

As a simple example, consider Person A regularly listens to music by Artist X and Artist Y. Another user, Person B, regularly listens to Artist Y and Artist Z.

With this data, a collaborative filtering algorithm can deduce, with some certainty, that Person A might enjoy being introduced to Artist Z, and Person B might enjoy the output of Artist X.

Of course, with millions of users and millions of songs, the matrix that is constructed to enable these suggestions to surface is considerably more complex than in this example, which is why AI algorithms are necessary to deliver these sorts of insights at scale.

It also looks for negative signals – skip a song within the first 30 seconds of it playing, and Spotify's AI algorithms will take that as a sign that you don't like it, and will give less weight to others similar to it in its recommendations.[4]

Spotify's recommendation engine goes further than that though, also utilizing audio analysis and natural language processing to create recommendations.

Audio analysis breaks down each individual track into its constituent parts – for example, tempo, beat, pitch of the notes, types of instruments and sounds used, and the prominence and pattern of lyrics.

This allows it to fine-tune its calculation of the probability that a certain user will like a particular track by comparing these elements to those of their favorite songs, as well as songs enjoyed by other users who match their listening preferences.

Natural language processing takes in external data – text found online relating to particular tracks. Spotify crawls the web to find news articles and blog posts that talk about tracks. It analyzes the sentiment of text describing each song – whether it is frequently described as "upbeat", "funky", "melancholy" or "heavy" – and uses this data to determine how receptive an individual user is likely to be to it.[5]

Spotify uses deep learning and neural nets to bring all of this information together and make recommendations it knows – to a high degree of probability – its users will love.[6]

How about if you let a friend borrow your login details? Well, it turns out that Spotify is well aware that a proportion of its members do this. So, its AI algorithms are smart enough to ignore drastic, but short-lived changes in listening habits.

Spotify does not have its own data centers – in 2018 it completed migration of its entire platform to Google Cloud. This allows it to scale more quickly without having to continuously upgrade its infrastructure to cope with new users coming on board.[7]

What Were The Results?

Spotify's Discover Weekly playlists mean that it is able to recommend new music that its users will love, and in return they are likely to remain as subscribers to the service.

Its success at predicting new music that users will love has been cited as a driving factor behind its success, with its subscriber base growing by 8 million, and share price rising by 25% in the three months following its listing on the New York Stock Exchange in April 2018.[8]

Key Challenges, Learning Points And Takeaways

- Big streaming services like Spotify have access to so much data that they can make highly accurate predictions, even about very personal and human issues such as our taste in music.

- Individual elements in a music track, such as the tempo, beat and content of lyrics, are good indicators that can be used to match it to listeners who will enjoy it.

- Amalgamating the results of analysis of several different datasets – user behavior, song data and external text data – allows Spotify's deep learning systems to produce increasingly accurate predictions.

- Presenting predictions to users in a way they will understand and feel comfortable with is often as important a factor as the predictions themselves – Spotify chose the Discover Weekly format because music is increasingly consumed through playlists.

Notes

1. Spotify, Spotify Technology S.A. Announces Financial Results for Second Quarter 2018: https://investors.spotify.com/financials/press-release-details/2018/Spotify-Technology-SA-Announces-Financial-Results-for-Second-Quarter-2018/default.aspx
2. YouTube, Vidhya Murali and Ching-wei Chen on predicting music: https://www.youtube.com/watch?time_continue=166&v=n5gCQWLXJcw
3. HPAC, Music Recommendation System Spotify: http://hpac.rwth-aachen.de/teaching/scm-mus-17/Reports/Madathil.pdf
4. Music:Ally, Spotify talks playlists, skip rates and NF's Nordic-fuelled success (#SlushMusic): https://musically.com/2017/11/29/spotify-playlists-skip-rates-nf/
5. Music Business Journal, Spotify's Secret Weapon: http://www.thembj.org/2014/10/spotifys-secret-weapon/
6. Quartz, The Magic That Makes Spotify's Discover Weekly Playlists So Damn Good: https://qz.com/571007/the-magic-that-makes-spotifys-discover-weekly-playlists-so-damn-good/
7. Computer World, How Spotify migrated everything from on-premise to Google Cloud Platform: https://www.computerworlduk.com/cloud-computing/how-spotify-migrated-everything-from-on-premise-google-cloud-platform-3681529/
8. Financial Times, Spotify gains 8m paid subscribers aided by Latin America growth: https://www.ft.com/content/16c0c91c-90cd-11e8-bb8f-a6a2f7bca546

27
TELEFONICA

Using Artificial Intelligence To Connect The Unconnected

Telefonica is a Spanish multinational telecom company, which is one of the largest telephone operators, broadband providers and mobile network providers in the world. In the United Kingdom it is known as O2 since the parent company acquired the brand, a spin-off from British Telecom, in 2006.

In 2018, it announced ambitious plans to connect up to 100 million inhabitants of some of the most remote regions of South America. It will do this by using artificial intelligence (AI) to locate communities underserved by telecoms infrastructure, and to allocate resources to enable them to be brought online.

What Problem Is Artificial Intelligence Trying To Solve?

Advanced technologies can do a lot to change people's lives for the better. Enhanced connectivity broadens opportunities and horizons for business and education, and allows vital services such as utilities and transport infrastructure to be planned and administered efficiently.

However, with more than half of the world's population still unable to access the internet,[1] vast swathes of the world are still unable to take advantage of these opportunities.

The problem is caused by the fact that while the cost of distributing online and connectivity infrastructure has fallen dramatically in urban areas, where there are large numbers of customers willing to pay for the services concentrated in relatively small geographic areas, in remote rural regions the story is very different.

Without high concentrations of people, the cost of rolling out connectivity infrastructure can be prohibitive. The problem is exacerbated by the fact that populations in remote regions are often difficult to track, and data on their movements and locations is limited, even today.

How Is Artificial Intelligence Used In Practice?

Telefonica's Internet Para Todos (Internet For All) project involves using AI to tackle the problem of rolling out online connectivity solutions to 100 million people living in remote regions of Latin America.

Latin America was chosen because 20% of the region's population still lack access to mobile broadband services, which can often play an essential part in social and economic development.[2]

By first using computer vision technology to study satellite images and understand where people are living, it was able to draw up plans to overcome the logistical difficulties inherent in connecting these isolated populations.

It was then able to analyze transport networks in the regions and use the data to optimize logistics of rolling out network coverage to reach as many people as possible. As remote rural areas are often poorly served by transport links such as roads and railways, deploying the necessary equipment to bring people online is generally the most expensive part of an operation to bring an area online.[3]

By comparing this information with data from its own network coverage, it was able to see which parts of the region were most in need of coverage, and where infrastructure could be rolled out with the greatest efficiency.

What Technology, Tools And Data Were Used?

Telefonica has partnered with Facebook for the Internet Para Todo project, which initially used machine learning analysis of high-definition satellite imagery to create maps showing where people are living.

It also uses satellite data to understand transport infrastructure links, as well as the Telefonica network's own data on the location of its transmitters and towers, and local census data.

The project incorporates plans for predictive maintenance – essential when it could take engineers days to reach locations where equipment has developed faults.[4]

Cooperation with local infrastructure operators, community organizers and entrepreneurs is an essential part of the scheme. Machine learning is used to process all of the data on the resources that are available and suggest solutions that have the potential to connect the largest number of people.

Together with Facebook, Telefonica is assessing technologies such as microwave and radio access network solutions, including Facebook's OpenCellular wireless connection platform, specifically engineered for bringing connectivity to isolated rural communities.

OpenCellular uses radio waves to transmit mobile broadband signals and is designed to take advantage of existing infrastructure such as towers, which may already be in place, dramatically reducing the cost of deployment.[5]

What Were The Results?

The machine learning and computer vision component of the program was able to map 95% of the population of the remote areas that were analyzed, with a less than 3% rate of false positives.[6]

A pilot scheme in Peru has already seen 10,000 residents of the Amazon basin connected to the internet.

Eventually, it is planned that up to 100 million could benefit. Connecting them to the internet will improve the economic outlook of entire communities, as well as give them access to modern healthcare and education resources for the first time.

This should lead to huge improvements in the quality of life of people who until now have not benefited from the technological advances that have reshaped much of the developed world.

Key Challenges, Learning Points And Takeaways

- Isolated populations have not benefited from the breakthroughs in communication technology enabled by the internet across the developed world.

- AI makes it possible to map population densities using satellite images to give more accurate data on where people are living.

- Analysis of transport infrastructure enables technology to be deployed in the most cost-effective way, making it viable to connect previously unreachable populations to the internet.

- Predictive maintenance makes it possible to understand when and how things are likely to break or require servicing, meaning repairs can be scheduled efficiently – this is essential when maintaining networks spread over large, sparsely inhabited regions.

Notes

1. ITU, ICT Facts and Figures 2016: https://www.itu.int/en/mediacentre/Pages/2016-PR30.aspx
2. Computer Weekly, MWC 2018: Telefónica aims to connect 100 million in Latin America: https://www.computerweekly.com/news/252435708/MWC-2018-Telefonica-aims-to-connect-100-million-in-Latin-America
3. LUCA, Ready For A Wild World: https://www.slideshare.net/wap13/big-data-for-social-good-106562070
4. Fierce Telecom, Telefónica's "Internet para Todos" project uses modern tools to find and connect Latin Americans: https://www.fiercetelecom.com/telecom/telefonica-s-internet-for-all-project-uses-modern-tools-to-find-and-connect-latin-americans
5. TechCrunch, Facebook's OpenCellular is a new open-source wireless access platform for remote areas: https://techcrunch.com/2016/07/06/facebooks-opencellular-is-a-new-open-source-wireless-access-platform-for-remote-areas/
6. Telefonica, How Telefónica uses artificial intelligence and machine learning to connect the unconnected: https://www.telefonica.com/en/web/public-policy/blog/article/-/blogs/how-telefonica-uses-artificial-intelligence-and-machine-learning-to-connect-the-unconnected

28
TWITTER

Using Artificial Intelligence To Fight Fake News And Spambots

There are over 330 million Twitter users using the social media platform to send hundreds of millions of tweets every day.[1]

People all around the world love the service for the ease it brings to staying in touch with friends, their favorite celebrities and keeping up to date with the news.

Unfortunately, due to the huge number of people using the service and its essentially anonymous nature, sometimes the news being pumped out 24/7 is fake. And sometimes the other people using the service may not have your best interests at heart.

One of the ways the social media giant uses artificial intelligence (AI) is to try to stay on top of the enormous challenge of keeping its users safe from those using it to spread harmful information.

What Problem Is Artificial Intelligence Helping To Solve?

The age of social media has given everyone a voice. And, as always, some people choose to use theirs to spread lies and misinformation.

Whether it's for political reasons or greed, since its birth social media has been a magnet for all types of scammers and propagandists, up to and including accusations of state-level electoral interference.[2]

While trolls targeting foreign elections may have made the headlines this year, more personal scamming is also rampant and often goes under the radar. A Gizmodo investigation found that fraudsters routinely steal photographs from innocent third parties to create fake accounts.[3]

Part of it is the inherent ease with which anybody can present themselves as anything. Just pick a name and an avatar and you have a safe shroud of anonymity from which you can spread anything from ponzi schemes to conspiracy theories and terrorist propaganda. An ongoing study by the Knight Foundation illustrates the problem as it identifies millions of fake news tweets being spread on Twitter.[4] Like most social networks, Twitter is keen to tackle this problem.

How Is Artificial Intelligence Used In Practice?

Since the rise in public awareness of the seriousness of fake news, Twitter has begun to take a more proactive stance towards identifying and removing offending accounts from its service.

Part of its strategy is to develop machine learning tools that can identify the networks of spambot accounts that fake news peddlers and scammers use to give their voice the illusion of legitimacy.[5]

This allows it to identify and shut down close to 10 million accounts every week, without having to wait until the accounts are reported by users.

It works by identifying patterns in an account's behavior – for example, linking to known fake news sites – and matching them with patterns displayed by known fake or bot accounts that were identified in the past.

Once an account has been highlighted as a possible offender, it is put into a read-only state, so its owner won't be able to use it to post.

Then Twitter asks the owner of the account to verify themselves as an actual human – with a phone number or legitimate email address.

Because fake news, conspiracy and scam networks operate by using hundreds or thousands of fake accounts to amplify their message, it often isn't feasible for the human operating the network to do this.

What Technology, Tools And Data Are Used?

Twitter has said that it does not want to publicly discuss the signs it uses to detect if an account is fake to hinder those who would try to develop workarounds.[6]

However, it is most likely that Twitter looks for accounts displaying patterns of activity that correlate with fake accounts identified in the past.

This is likely to include posting frequency, networking behavior (who the account follows and unfollows), large numbers of accounts appearing to originate from a limited number of IP addresses and the use of technology such as VPN to obscure identity and geographical location.

When accounts following particular patterns around those activities also seem to be consistently sharing content from websites identified as untrustworthy or dishonest, there's a higher probability that they could be fake accounts.

Twitter's involvement with AI technology is certainly not limited to dealing with fake accounts. The platform also uses deep learning to decide how interesting particular tweets will be to individual users, and the prominence they should receive in their timeline.[7]

It does this by analyzing every individual tweet from the accounts that a user follows, and assessing it based on how popular it is, the user's prior interactions with the author and how well it matches features of other tweets you have interacted with in the past.

Many of Twitter's initiatives are directed by Cortex, its in-house specialist AI team.

What Were The Results?

In two months, Twitter used automated detection tools to take down more than 70 million "fake and suspicious" accounts.[8]

Year on year, 214% more accounts have been removed for violating spam policies. At the same time, reports from users that they have encountered spam dropped from 25,000 per day in March 2018 to 17,000 per day in May 2018. Twitter points to this as evidence that its proactive policy is removing spam and fake accounts from its platform before users even see them.[9]

As well as social good, the initiative by Twitter to drop fake users from its system serves a business purpose. Advertisers want to know the ads they pay to show on Twitter are being seen by real people, not bots.

Key Challenges, Learning Points And Takeaways

- Scammers and those with malicious intent can be identified by their behavior online using AI, employing very similar techniques to those used by marketers to decide who to target ads to.

- Sometimes anonymity is important. Because Twitter understands that occasionally asking for accounts to identify themselves may restrict free speech in ways that could be dangerous, it operates a trust and safety council.[10]

- Twitter realizes that the freedom of speech its platform offers is important, but has put its belief that the safety of users is paramount at the top of its agenda.

Notes

1. Twitter, How policy changes work: https://blog.twitter.com/official/en_us/topics/company/2017/HowPolicyChangesWork.html
2. Financial Times, Senate panel backs finding of Russian meddling in US election: https://www.ft.com/content/04385510-7f13-11e8-8e67-1e1a0846c475
3. Gizmodo, The Bizarre Scheme Using Viral Abuse Stories and Stolen Pics to Sell Diet Pills on Twitter: https://gizmodo.com/the-bizarre-scheme-using-viral-abuse-stories-and-stolen-1829173964
4. Knight Foundation, Disinformation, "Fake News" and Influence Campaigns on Twitter: https://www.knightfoundation.org/reports/disinformation-fake-news-and-influence-campaigns-on-twitter
5. Twitter, How Twitter is Fighting Spam and Malicious Automation: https://blog.twitter.com/official/en_us/topics/company/2018/how-twitter-is-fighting-spam-and-malicious-automation.html
6. Twitter, Our approach to bots and misinformation: https://blog.twitter.com/official/en_us/topics/company/2017/Our-Approach-Bots-Misinformation.html
7. Twitter, Using Deep Learning at Scale in Twitter's Timelines: https://blog.twitter.com/engineering/en_us/topics/insights/2017/using-deep-learning-at-scale-in-twitters-timelines.html
8. Washington Post, Twitter is sweeping out fake accounts like never before, putting user growth at risk: https://www.washingtonpost.com/technology/2018/07/06/twitter-is-sweeping-out-fake-accounts-like-never-before-putting-user-growth-risk
9. Twitter, How Twitter is fighting spam and malicious automation: https://blog.twitter.com/official/en_us/topics/company/2018/how-twitter-is-fighting-spam-and-malicious-automation.html
10. Twitter, Announcing the Twitter Trust & Safety Council: https://blog.twitter.com/official/en_us/a/2016/announcing-the-twitter-trust-safety-council.html

29
VERIZON

Using Machine Learning To Assess Service Quality

Verizon started life as one of the "baby Bells", coming into existence initially as Bell Atlantic when the US Justice Department forced the breaking up of the Bell telephone conglomerate in 1984.

Today, as Verizon Communications, it is one of the largest communication technology companies in the world. It is the No. 1 provider of wireless subscription services in the United States[1] and it offers high-speed fibre optic broadband services to millions of US subscribers through its Fios service.[2]

Until recently, Verizon's main source of data on how well the network was running and the quality of service experienced by its users came from customer feedback.

It now monitors traffic and data across its network and uses machine learning to understand how service quality is affected by usage spikes, as well as external factors such as the weather and changing customer habits.

Verizon brought additional machine learning expertise into the business through its acquisition of Yahoo! in 2017.

What Problem Is Artificial Intelligence Helping To Solve?

Monitoring a network of the scale of Verizon's to understand where faults and outages occur takes a monumental amount of effort.

Traditionally, this has been done through customer feedback – essentially waiting for something to go wrong and the complaints about poor service to start flooding in.

It was only possible to react to problems after they occur – meaning that even if Verizon was able to find the cause and fix it, customers had already experienced a drop in their quality of service.

Being able to predict where problems arise before they affect customers would be preferable, but until machine learning was sufficiently advanced, the analytics tools needed to make such accurate predictions were available.

How Is Artificial Intelligence Used In Practice?

Verizon's machine learning algorithms crunch data gathered from all of its network elements and use the insights to understand how and when outages and faults occur.

This means that it is able to recognize when situations are occurring that are similar to those that have caused network problems in the past – for example, spikes in customer data use, or extreme weather conditions that could lead to equipment failure.

It does this by analyzing all of the factors available and establishing "normal" levels of operation. It then looks for indicators of outliers – events that fall outside of normal patterns of behavior – and attempts to establish their cause.

Verizon's director of network performance and analytics, Matt Tegerdine, told me: "The beauty of this is that we don't just look at one singular data source like interface statistics – we're also going out and collecting things like environmental statistics, CPU usage on routers – we use machine learning to learn what 'normal' is."

The aim is to listen to as many network elements as possible and then use predictive modelling to ensure that customers receive an interruption-free service wherever possible.

In fact, customer satisfaction is the metric that underpins the entire strategy, with reducing customer "churn" – the number of customers who do not renew their subscription – the priority.

Verizon has also introduced a chatbot that operates through Facebook Messenger. Customers are able to use the familiar conversational interface they use to chat with their friends to ask natural language questions about what's on television, get technical advice such as information on how to reset their router and ask for up-to-date billing information.[3]

What Technology, Tools And Data Were Used?

Tegerdine told me: "It's a very complex ecosystem of different data sources, and it's that combination that drives a lot of insights and is where the value of the analytics increases."

In fact, Verizon's predictive analytics algorithms monitor 3 GB of data every second, streamed from millions of network interfaces, customer routers, sensors that gather temperature and weather data, and operational data, which includes customer billing records.

Verizon's chatbot uses natural language processing and neural net technology to answer customer questions through Facebook's Messenger platform.

What Were The Results?

In 2017, Verizon predicted 200 "customer impacting" events before they happened, thanks to its machine learning-driven predictive technology.[4]

Because of this, these issues were remedied before they caused a problem to its customers.

The telecoms giant was also able to use insights generated through its network monitoring platform to drive business and marketing decisions. Through the extensive monitoring and testing of the service, engineers were surprised to learn that their 750 MB/s service was actually consistently providing speeds of 1 GB/s into customers' homes. This meant they were able to rebrand their service as a 1 GB service, leading to a noticeable increase in sales.[5]

Key Challenges, Learning Points And Takeaways

- Predicting customer-impacting events means that they can be fixed before they cause issues, leading to higher customer satisfaction and reduced churn rates.

- The size and reach of Verizon's network mean that there is a wealth of data available that can be used to predict these events.

- The fact that much of Verizon's data is internal data and not available to other businesses gives it a competitive advantage.

Notes

1. Recode, A merged T-Mobile and Sprint will still be smaller than AT&T or Verizon: https://www.recode.net/2018/4/30/17300652/tmobile-sprint-att-verizon-merger-wireless-subscriber-chart
2. Verizon Fios: https://www.verizon.com/home/fios/
3. Knowledge@Wharton, Tapping AI: The Future of Customer Experience at Verizon Fios: http://knowledge.wharton.upenn.edu/article/competing-with-the-disruptors-a-view-of-future-customer-experience-at-verizon-fios/
4. Verizon, How Verizon is using artificial intelligence and machine learning to help maintain network superiority: https://www.verizon.com/about/our-company/fourth-industrial-revolution/how-verizon-using-artificial-intelligence-and-machine-learning-help-maintain-network
5. Forbes, The Amazing Ways Verizon Uses AI And Machine Learning To Improve Performance: https://www.forbes.com/sites/bernardmarr/2018/06/22/the-amazing-ways-verizon-uses-ai-and-machine-learning-to-improve-performance/#2b859af07638

30
VIACOM

Using Artificial Intelligence To Stream Videos
Faster And Improve Customer Experience

Viacom is a vast media network, which as well as taking in household name brands such as Nickelodeon, Comedy Central and MTV, spans 400 YouTube channels, 60 Instagram pages, 430 Facebook pages and 100 Twitter handles.

It has invested heavily in real-time analytics across its networks, using artificial intelligence (AI) platforms to draw out insights that it can use to improve the customer experience.

What Problem Is Artificial Intelligence Helping To Solve?

With so many channels – taking in both TV brands and social media – data is plentiful regarding customer viewing habits, preferences and convenience. Making sense of all of that data can be tricky. A business like Viacom needs to understand how every variable, from Facebook posts "likes" to the time it takes to launch a streaming video, impacts on the amount of time viewers will spend with it.

It also has to ensure there is sufficient bandwidth availability to pump its content out to its customers around the world. Getting this wrong can lead to buffering and stutter during video playback – a factor that is very likely to get customers looking elsewhere for their entertainment.

Viacom's senior director of product analytics, Dan Morris, told me: "Delivery of video is at the core of everything we do, and our goal is to be exceptional at that.

"But there are a lot of variables at play – we have internal systems talking to external systems, we have content delivery, we have ad servers, and on the user side there's a whole bunch of environmental factors like wi-fi connectivity which we really have no control over."

How Is Artificial Intelligence Used In Practice?

Viacom used network data and social media signals to understand as much as possible about how its audience consumed its services. From this it was able to determine its "North Star" metric – the most important target to achieve to hit its goals.

Facebook in its early days deduced through running analytics on its users' behavior that if it could get them connected to seven friends within 10 days, they were likely to become long-term users of the platform.[1]

Viacom's North Star metric turned out to be that customers who were hooked on two or more shows had a 350% more likely chance of becoming loyal, long-term viewers of Viacom output.

By persuading them to watch four shows regularly, that probability leapt up to 700%.

This insight means the company was able to dedicate more resources to persuading customers who are already enjoying one show to also watch a second, third or fourth.

Long-term, loyal viewers who look to Viacom's properties first when looking to spend some time viewing content are what attract advertisers to the network, and generate the company's revenue.

Viacom also uses AI algorithms to monitor the flow of data and available bandwidth across its online streaming video platforms.

The quality of its video feeds is constantly monitored to understand where customers are receiving poor service.

Here, it was able to ascertain that two variables had the highest impact on whether customers would continue to watch. These were "time to first frame" – how long the video took to start playing – and the rebuffering rate – how frequently the video stutters during playback to load more data.

By using AI-driven analytics to reroute bandwidth availability to keep these two metrics at optimum levels, Viacom enhances its customers' experience.

What Technology, Tools And Data Were Used?

Viacom put together a seven-person data science team to orchestrate automated data capture and analytics across its hundreds of social media channels.[2]

It now has a tool that pulls information from social networks as frequently as every five minutes, monitoring the performance of content marketing posts promoting its brands, driving traffic to its websites or suggesting customers "tune in" to popular shows.

"Social war rooms" are established around all of the network's "tentpole" shows to understand how its viewers' experience is affected by variables that can be influenced through social media – such as post engagement rates, timing and choice of channel.[3]

To monitor and analyze network signals that allow it to observe the behavior of its streaming video playback, Viacom built another platform utilizing machine learning, using Apache Spark and Databricks, running on Amazon Web Services.[4]

The system proactively monitors video feed quality and automatically allocates resources when user experience drops below optimal levels.

What Were The Results?

Viacom's social media analytics platform helps it to measure the impact posting different content at different times of the day and on different networks has on customer viewing habits.

It helps Viacom to distribute the resources at its disposal for promoting content – for example, social influencers – where the analytics suggests they will positively affect metrics – such as the number of shows a customer enjoys.

Through its Databricks system, Viacom was able to drive an overall reduction of 33% in the time it takes streaming videos to start when played over its web services. This improvement in viewer experience was shown to increase customer retention and drive brand loyalty.

Key Challenges, Learning Points And Takeaways

- The impact of social signals such as post engagement can be demystified with AI, and their impact on core business processes more deeply understood.

- Social media offers unparalleled opportunity to get to know your customer, but you may need advanced tools such as AI to cut through all of the noise and find the insights that matter.

- AI is now powerful enough to implement real-time monitoring and automate resource management across vast data networks, such as Viacom's streaming video output.

- Identifying a key driver of success – a North Pole metric – is a primary use case for many AI analytics initiatives in business.

Notes

1. Startup Marketing, How Chamath Palihapitiya put Facebook on the path to 1 billion users: https://ryangum.com/chamath-palihapitiya-how-we-put-facebook-on-the-path-to-1-billion-users
2. Digiday, How Viacom uses artificial intelligence to predict the success of its social campaigns: https://digiday.com/media/viacom-uses-artificial-intelligence-predict-success-social-campaigns/
3. Digiday, How Viacom uses artificial intelligence to predict the success of its social campaigns: https://digiday.com/media/viacom-uses-artificial-intelligence-predict-success-social-campaigns/
4. Databricks, Customer Case Study, Viacom: https://databricks.com/wp-content/uploads/2018/04/viacom case study.pdf

Part 4
SERVICES, FINANCIAL AND HEALTHCARE COMPANIES

31
AMERICAN EXPRESS

Using Artificial Intelligence To Detect Fraud And Improve Customer Experience

American Express handles more than 25% of US credit card spending, accounting for $1.1 trillion of transactions in 2017,[1] and is the world's most valuable financial services brand according to Forbes.[2]

The company puts data and analytics, driven by machine learning, at the heart of everything it does; however, two of its key use cases are detecting fraud and improving customer experience.

What Problem Is Artificial Intelligence Helping To Solve?

Global credit card fraud causes losses of around $20 billion to businesses and customers every year.[3] This often takes the form of card not present fraud when stolen or forged details are used to purchase goods or services over the internet or telephone.

Card payment processing systems must be built to handle large volumes of transactions every minute of every day to be useful to businesses and consumers. This means attempts at fraud must be detected quickly and there is only a small window of opportunity to do so. Incorrectly flagging up valid transactions as fraudulent is inconvenient for customers, and if it happens too often, they will look to other methods of payment to avoid the hassle.

As fraudsters are often technologically adept themselves, they have developed and deployed high-tech systems of their own to circumvent anti-fraud security systems. This can include "spoofing" location data to make it appear to security systems that transactions are originating from a different part of the world, or identity fraud to make it appear that a trusted customer is behind a particular transaction.

An "arms race" has been ongoing for decades as banks and fraudsters seek to outsmart each other. Artificial intelligence (AI) represents the latest evolution of this competition, and while fraud will almost certainly always exist, banks and credit card companies hope they can use technology to give their customers the confidence they need to conduct business through their networks.

How Is Artificial Intelligence Used In Practice?

Banks and other financial institutions such as card issuers and insurers have always used patterns presented in historical data to attempt to detect fraud. Examples include watching out for cardholders making uncharacteristically high-value transactions, or transactions that appear to originate from outside their home country.

Transactions, once found to be fraudulent, are logged, and characteristics are flagged as possible indicators that can be used to suggest future transactions may also be fraudulent. The personal details of the person making the transaction, the place where the transaction originates and the suppliers, goods and services involved are all potential indicators.

These allowed financial institutions to build models that can be used to predict the trustworthiness of future transactions, but they are cumbersome to build and often could only be updated with new information infrequently rather than in real time.[4]

American Express has built AI systems that are able to read in data from card transactions around the world in real time as they happen. This means fraudulent characteristics can be logged and fed back into detection algorithms almost in real time. Having access to far more data means more complex patterns of characteristics can be examined.

This means that even if fraudsters are able to spoof or fake certain characteristics of the transaction, there's a better chance that algorithms will detect anomalies in other characteristics quickly enough to warn that the transaction is suspect.

Aside from this, American Express also uses machine learning in several ways that are designed to improve the customer experience by giving added value to card users. One example is through its acquisition of AI-driven "personal travel assistant" app, Mezi.[5]

The idea here is that as well as helping you to securely spend money, AI assistants built into card apps can help you decide where to spend it by offering personalized recommendations based on your habits and previous purchase history – much like a recommendation engine of the type used by Amazon and other online retailers.

What Technology, Tools And Data Were Used?

Data primarily comes from historical transaction records as well as information gathered about individual customers when they sign up to become American Express cardholders.

Using machine learning to spot fraud among the millions of transactions occurring every day requires sophisticated storage solutions that are able to cope with ingesting and making available large volumes of data. To achieve this, American Express uses a Hadoop-based distributed storage infrastructure.[6]

Using traditional computer storage infrastructure, it just wouldn't be possible to access enough historical transactional data quickly enough to make an accurate prediction in an acceptably short timeframe.

American Express's fraud detection systems used a combination of supervised and unsupervised learning techniques to become increasingly efficient at raising flags when data indicative of fraudulent transactions is encountered.

What Were The Results?

Analyzing transactions in real time using machine learning algorithms means that there is a greater chance that fraudulent transactions will be detected.

It also means there is less chance of false positives occurring, which are inconvenient for customers and may make them less willing to trust the American Express payment system for making their transactions.

More fraudulent transactions will be blocked as they occur, meaning it is less likely that remedial action, such as recovering spent funds, will have to be taken after the fact, drastically reducing the costs involved in dealing with fraud.

Key Challenges, Learning Points And Takeaways

- Machine learning models for detecting fraud need to constantly adapt and update themselves in real time, meaning they need a consistent flow of data to learn from.

- Distributed storage and large amounts of compute power are needed to handle the amount of data that is needed to make accurate predictions in real time.

- The large number of transactions processed by American Express means that small increases in efficiency can make big improvements to overall security.

- As well as fraud detection, financial services businesses are looking to AI for the added value it can give to customers, leading to changes in the way they can access their services.

Notes

1. American Express, Company 2018 Investor Day: http://ir.american-express.com/Cache/1001233287.PDF?O=PDF&T=&Y=&D=&FID=1001233287&iid=102700
2. Forbes, The World's Most Valuable Brands: https://www.forbes.com/powerful-brands/list/
3. The Nilson Report, Card Fraud Losses: https://nilsonreport.com/upload/content_promo/The_Nilson_Report_Issue_1118.pdf
4. Mapr, New Age Fraud Analytics: Machine Learning on Hadoop: https://mapr.com/blog/new-age-fraud-analytics-machine-learning-hadoop/
5. American Express, American Express Acquires Mezi: https://about.americanexpress.com/press-release/american-express-acquires-mezi
6. Mapr, Machine Learning at American Express: Benefits and Requirements: https://mapr.com/blog/machine-learning-american-express-benefits-and-requirements/

32
ELSEVIER

Using Artificial Intelligence To Improve Medical Decisions And Scientific Research

Elsevier is a global multimedia publishing business that offers more than 20,000 products for educational and professional science and healthcare communities, including leading research publications such as *The Lancet* and *Cell*.

Stage one of the company's ongoing digital transformation has involved the digitization of the huge amount of data published in reports and journals during the company's 140-year history.

Now it is building artificial intelligence (AI) tools that will draw new insights from this data, as well as combining it with other big data sources such as anonymized patient data and data from insurance claims.

What Problem Is Artificial Intelligence Helping To Solve?

In the United States, it can often be the case that two patients of the same age and gender will present to their primary healthcare practitioner with the same symptoms, and yet there will be a huge variation in the outcome, and cost, of the treatment they receive.[1]

This is because diagnosing and treating are done by different health-care staff with different levels of knowledge and experience, as well as personal feelings about which treatments are more effective and how to achieve preferred outcomes.

By developing AI-derived "pathways" from initial presentation and examination to treatment procedures and prescribing of medication, patients are more likely to get better quicker, and the cost of providing healthcare is reduced.

How Is Artificial Intelligence Used In Practice?

Elsevier is building what it calls its advanced clinical decision support platform, which uses natural language processing and machine learning to suggest the optimal treatment pathway for patients.

The system builds on its Via Oncology platform, which is currently deployed in leading cancer centers around the United States. It is able to correlate data from patient records as well as Elsevier's vast archive of research published through its medical journals.

It then looks for previous cases where patients have reported the same sets of symptoms, and analyzes what outcomes were achieved. It is then able to suggest the treatment that is most likely, based on the data, to have a positive outcome for the patient.

I spoke to John Danaher, president of clinical solutions at Elsevier, who told me that moving forward with development of platforms that combine AI analytics with their vast data sources is currently a key business priority.

Elsevier used all of its content – books, journal articles, etc. – to map diseases to symptoms, which allowed it to create predictive models. The company then trained its neural network models against large patient databases to create models that can generate a differential diagnosis. The model can then give weighted predictions that these particular symptoms in a person of this age and gender give you a 70% chance it's disease A or a 35% chance it's disease B.

What Tools, Technology And Data Were Used?

Elsevier's platform uses anonymized patient data, including medical histories, treatment histories and outcomes. It also uses a database of 5 million medical insurance claims. Then it throws in all of the articles and research published in its journals over the last 140 years.

To carry out analysis on this data it has built its own proprietary analytics tools. These tools utilize natural language processing to understand the contents of the medical literature in its database, as well as the patient records.

The company is evaluating commercial big data and AI solutions such as those offered by Microsoft and Amazon for the next stage of its AI rollout, Danaher tells me.

As well as its advanced clinical decision support platform, Elsevier applies AI to research solutions outside of the healthcare ecosphere, such as its Science Direct tool. This tool also uses the published corpus of scientific literature, and supports researchers by pointing them in the direction of relevant publications and articles that the AI predicts will be relevant to their work.[2]

What Were The Results?

The best indicator of the results, says Danaher, is the adherence rate of 85% among clinical staff to the treatment pathways suggested by its Via Oncology platform.

He says: "You want to know that if you go to MD Anderson, you're going to get the most current care given to you by the smartest tools – oh, and by the way, that you're going to get the best outcomes.

"So, we get over 85% adherence to our pathways by our clinicians, and when they do go off pathway, which happens sometimes – patients may have allergies to certain medicines – we review and look at the reasons for them going off pathway and if necessary review our decision making.

"You can see the ramifications for how people will do clinical research in the future too – it's all going to be driven by these analytics."

Key Challenges, Learning Points And Takeaways

- Elsevier amalgamates patient medical records, insurance claims and billing data and published medical literature to predict which treatment pathways are most likely to be effective.

- Elsevier owns 25% of the US output of published scientific and medical research. It has looked to AI to develop new methods of drawing value from this information.

- Treatment can be standardized if machines are used to determine optimal treatment paths dependent on the patient's details, medical history and the symptoms they present with.

- Standardized treatments lead to better patient outcomes if they can be optimized according to data, and also help healthcare providers to reduce overall costs.

Notes

1. Wall Street Journal, Mayo Clinic's Unusual Challenge: Overhaul a Business That's Working: https://www.wsj.com/articles/mayo-clinics-unusual-challenge-overhaul-a-business-thats-working-1496415044

2. LinkedIn, Artificial Intelligence And Big Data: The Amazing Digital Transformation Of Elsevier From Publisher To Tech Company: https://www.linkedin.com/pulse/artificial-intelligence-big-data-amazing-digital-elsevier-marr/

33
ENTRUPY

Using Artificial Intelligence To Combat The $450 Billion Counterfeit Industry

Launched in 2016, Entrupy uses artificial intelligence (AI) to combat counterfeit goods. The company provides its platform as a service to brands that want to minimize revenue lost to counterfeiters, as well as resellers who want to ensure they aren't inadvertently breaking the law by selling fake goods.

CEO and co-founder Vidyuth Srinivasan said he settled on counterfeiting as the focus of his machine learning development, following a battery failure on an apparently new and genuine battery while motor biking across the country.[1]

What Problem Is Artificial Intelligence Helping To Solve?

Aside from dodgy batteries, sales of counterfeit goods total close to half a trillion dollars per year globally.[2] As well as revenue lost to the brands whose IP is being stolen, this dilutes brand identities – something fashion brands in particular are more than willing to spend money to protect.

Counterfeiting also eats into the business of genuine resellers and wholesalers and sometimes leaves them out of pocket when stock purchased in good faith turns out to be fake. A widely used style of fraud known as return fraud involves dishonestly returning counterfeit items to retailers in place of genuine ones. This is only possible because many retailers don't have the time or technological means to check every item that comes back to them.

How Is Artificial Intelligence Used In Practice?

Entrupy has developed scanning technology that uses machine learning and deep learning techniques[3] to detect whether items are genuine. Clothes, accessories, jewellery, electrical goods and even automobile parts can be "fingerprinted" in minute detail. Service users can then use either a phone app or a dedicated handheld scanner to check if their purchases, or inventory, are the real deal.

This is possible thanks to microscope cameras that are able to record the tiniest details of a product's construction, such as the direction of tiny microfibres during the weaving process and the use of deep learning algorithms to assess a potentially counterfeited product. Any scanned image can be compared in real time to the reference images stored in the cloud to provide an immediate assessment as to whether it is genuine or not.

Entrupy claims that its technology is able to discern even "super fakes" – very high-quality replicas that are impossible for a human to differentiate from a genuine product.

What Technology, Tools And Data Were Used?

Entrupy has a database of millions of images[4] of products sold by the brands it covers, which include Chanel, Dior, Burberry, Gucci, Louis

Vuitton and Prada – some of the most counterfeited names in the world.

Specialized microscope lenses were needed for capturing the training images, as most microscopes aren't capable of capturing both the level of detail and the required amount of surface area for the data to be usable.

The images of the genuine products are used to train convolutional neural network algorithms to classify images based on texture, differences in threads and grains and marks made on products during manufacturing.[5] On second-hand goods it can even distinguish differences in wear and tear to identify a fake product.

What Were The Results?

Entrupy say that its system has a 98.5%[6] rate of correctly identifying counterfeit merchandise.

This means that as the technology becomes more widely used, retailers and customers will be able to buy more confidently, and the lives of counterfeiters will become more difficult.

Key Challenges, Learning Points And Takeaways

- AI can parse image data in incredibly high detail far more quickly than a human eye could, and determine between counterfeit products and genuine items.

- Brands are happy to help with putting this technology into the hands of customers and resellers if it helps protect their revenue and perceived value.

- Counterfeiting has existed throughout human history and is unlikely ever to be completely eradicated. As with other types of fraudsters, counterfeiters are likely to step up their own technology game in response.

- AI start-ups that build their business models on creating unique datasets will increasingly be seen as valuable allies to large corporations that can find value in that data.

Notes

1. Tech.co, How AI Is Powering the Fight Against the $900B Counterfeit Industry: https://tech.co/ai-counterfeits-2017-08
2. OECD, 2018 – Trade in Counterfeit and Pirated Goods.
3. Entrupy.com: https://www.entrupy.com/technology/
4. Tech Crunch, Machine learning can tell if you're wearing swap-meet Louie: https://techcrunch.com/2017/08/11/machine-learning-can-tell-if-youre-wearing-swap-meet-louie/
5. KDD, The Fake vs Real Goods Problem: Microscopy and Machine Learning to the Rescue, Ashlesh Sharma, Vidyuth Srinivasan, Vishal Kanchan, Lakshminarayanan Subramanian: http://delivery.acm.org/10.1145/3100000/3098186/p2011-sharma.pdf
6. Entrupy.com: https://www.entrupy.com/

34
EXPERIAN

Using Artificial Intelligence To Make Mortgages Simpler

Experian is one of the world's largest consumer credit reference agencies, which means that businesses, banks and financial institutions rely on its help to decide, for example, whether we are a safe bet to lend money to.

It also means it holds a huge amount of data on us and our spending habits. Now it is applying artificial intelligence (AI) to this data to make more accurate predictions, but also to make our lives easier when it comes to complex financial transactions.

One area where it is concentrating its efforts is mortgages, and it hopes that by using machine learning it will cut down the time it takes to complete the lengthy process of applying for mortgages, leading to less stress and lower fees.

What Problem Is Artificial Intelligence Helping To Solve?

Applying for a mortgage is a time-consuming and complex process. The average application involves coordinating information between a large number of agencies – buyers, sellers, surveyors, estate agents, solicitors, underwriters, mortgage brokers and lenders.[1]

This is the reason why buying a property is often listed as one of the most stressful life events that we deal with.

Often work is duplicated between agencies due to inconsistencies in the way information is transferred, and of course that leads to higher fees, adding to the overall expense of the process to us as consumers.

Although the process has been streamlined to some extent due to adoption of digital technology in recent decades, the reality is that it will still take weeks, even months, to get a mortgage approved,[2] involving several days' worth of activity and visits to numerous offices and agencies.

How Is Artificial Intelligence Used In Practice?

Experian is trialling an AI system that will work by analyzing thousands of mortgage applications to determine where efficiencies can be made by reducing duplicate workloads and streamlining workflows between different parties.[3]

The system will be trained to look at each data element, assess how frequently it is used during the process and categorize it so it can be quickly located and passed to where it is needed.

This type of work would be practically impossible for a human to carry out on anything other than a small historic sample dataset. Machines, on the other hand, can work on fast-flowing real-time data, which is updated every time a new mortgage application is completed.

It's also possible that this form of predictive technology will make it easier for those with limited credit histories to obtain mortgages or personal loans. Lenders will be able to assess applications based on data of other customers that fits the applicant's profile, and come to more accurate and trustworthy decisions about their ability to keep up payments.[4]

What Technology, Tools And Data Were Used?

Machine learning is used to process data across the workflow. As it learns more about where data is used, and in some cases isn't used, it can build accurate models about what data is valuable, and what is surplus to requirements, at each stage of the process.

As Experian CIO Barry Libenson put it when I talked to him: "Over time we may find out that we don't need to care about five years' worth of tax returns – what we need is five years of credit payments."

Experian has built a platform that it calls Analytic Sandbox, which allows it to produce on-demand data-driven insights. It used the open source H20 machine learning and deep learning framework to drive its analytics algorithms.[5]

It also uses Cloudera's Enterprise platform to enable quick access to big data, helping it to make more accurate decisions based on consumers' credit histories.[6]

What Were The Results?

Libenson told me that the process will be ready to roll out in 2018/2019. When it does, it is expected that it could reduce the time it takes to have a mortgage application approved from weeks or months to a matter of days.[7]

Shortly after that – by 2021 or 2022, he estimates – "We will find that the datasets we are using will be quite different from the ones we initially used."

In the long term, it should mean that consumers' lives are simplified, and businesses benefit from being able to make more accurate, data-driven decisions.

In real terms, it should also mean we end up paying lower fees to the various agencies involved with the compliance and approval elements of the process, due to less need for them to duplicate work already carried out by other agencies.

Key Challenges, Learning Points And Takeaways

- Credit reference agencies are ideally positioned to streamline workflows across complex procedures such as mortgages, due to their function as the contact point between multiple agencies.

- AI means every aspect of the workflow can be examined and tracked in detail across a large number of instances, and areas where efficiencies can be made will become apparent.

- Smart businesses are learning that repackaging data, processing it with machine learning and offering it as a service is a great way of diversifying their range of services in the age of AI.

- Implementing systems such as this inevitably opens new security risks. One challenge is ensuring that security is in place. As Libenson puts it: "The trick here is to not let the technology get ahead of the security. We have to spend as much time and energy focused on making sure the ecosystem is secure as we do delivering the service. Doing that on a global basis…adds another layer of complexity."

Notes

1. Home Buyers Institute, Why Do Mortgage Lenders Take So Long to Process and Approve Loans?: http://www.homebuyinginstitute.com/mortgage/why-do-lenders-take-so-long/

2. Realtor, How Long Does It Take to Get a Mortgage? Longer Than You Might Think: https://www.realtor.com/advice/finance/how-long-does-it-take-to-get-a-mortgage/
3. Forbes, How Experian Is Using Big Data And Machine Learning To Cut Mortgage Application Times To A Few Days: https://www.forbes.com/sites/bernardmarr/2017/05/25/how-experian-is-using-big-data-and-machine-learning-to-cut-mortgage-application-times-to-a-few-days/#7869322f203f
4. Tech Emergence, Artificial Intelligence Applications for Lending and Loan Management: https://www.techemergence.com/artificial-intelligence-applications-lending-loan-management/
5. Experian, Bringing Machine Learning to Data Analytics: http://www.experian.com/blogs/insights/2017/05/machine-learning-with-analytical-sandbox/
6. Experian, Experian selects Cloudera to deliver instant access to aggregated financial data: https://www.experianplc.com/media/ncws/2017/experian-selects-cloudera-to-deliver-instant-access-to-aggregated-financial-data/
7. Forbes, How Experian Is Using Big Data And Machine Learning To Cut Mortgage Application Times To A Few Days: https://www.forbes.com/sites/bernardmarr/2017/05/25/how-cxperian-is-using-big-data-and-machine-learning-to-cut-mortgage-application-times-to-a-few-days/#7869322f203f

35
HARLEY-DAVIDSON

Using Artificial Intelligence To Increase Sales

Harley-Davidson is an American manufacturer of motorcycles, which sells around 150,000[1] bikes around the world each year. It also licenses its iconic brand for use on clothing, homeware and accessories. The bikes are sold through its worldwide network of dealerships. The owner of Harley-Davidson New York, Asaf Jacobi, was walking in Riverside Park wondering how he could get out of a sales slump when he met Or Shani, CEO of artificial intelligence (AI) marketing specialists Adgorithm.

What Problem Is Artificial Intelligence Helping To Solve?

When you think of Harley-Davidson you may not initially think of a high-tech business. In fact, its bikes are still individually assembled by humans on the shop floor – to ensure a level of bespoke and custom detail that fully automated assembly lines are still not able to deliver.

Selling expensive, high-end goods such as cars or motorcycles is a low-volume business – Harley-Davidson New York was averaging one or two sales per week.[2] In this type of business, it's worth spending money to attract customers, as every sale makes a noticeable impression on the bottom line – but it's important that money is being spent on attracting the right customers.

Understanding how to most effectively use a marketing budget is essential, but without the right data, determining who, and where, your customers are can be hit and miss. Once you've got that data, you need to understand it, and humans just aren't that great at combing through terabytes of statistical and demographic data to spot correlations.

How Is Artificial Intelligence Used In Practice?

To attract new customers, marketers work to understand their existing customers, find more people who match a similar profile and then spend their marketing budgets on putting advertising or promotions in front of them.

AI makes this process far more efficient. Because of their immense speed and processing power, computer algorithms can ingest customer (or potential customer) data far more quickly, and spot patterns and correlations that would never be seen by a human analyst. Once a machine learning algorithm has spotted such a pattern, and learned that it is a successful indicator of a potential lead, it can train itself to focus more intently on spotting that particular pattern when it emerges again.

We've got used to this behavior from the likes of Amazon and Google, but as its usefulness has become apparent, a market has emerged in which numerous start-ups and established names such as Salesforce have begun developing their own algorithms to offer "as a service" to corporate clients. This has led to companies that are perhaps not best known for their adoption of cutting-edge technology integrating AI – often starting with their sales operations.

What Technology, Tools And Data Were Used?

Harley-Davidson New York used Adgorithm's Albert platform to segment its customer profiles and audience base, and more accurately identify potential buyers.

Albert monitored data such as customers' buying habits, the areas of the webpage they viewed and the length of time they spent viewing the site to identify patterns among those who would go on to make expensive purchases.

It then found people whose patterns fitted the mould, and conducted market research with them, asking them to respond to different combinations of advertising words and imagery. After hitting on the winning formula, it scoured online ad networks such as Google Ads, Facebook and Bing,[3] looking for customers matching the profile, and putting the adverts that had proven most effective in front of them.

What Were The Results?

After moving to AI-driven customer targeting, Harley-Davidson New York increased its lead generation by 2,930%. As well as vastly increasing sales (it sold more than twice its previous record during the first weekend), it opened the company up to entirely new audiences that it had never previously marketed to.

It also discovered that Facebook was by far its most effective advertising channel – with ads placed there converting 8.5 times higher than other channels – so the company took the decision to increase resources there.

Another key finding was that customers responded far better to the word "call" in adverts than "buy" – 447% better, in fact. The AI system was able to recognize this in real time and adapt its language on the fly, as it posted adverts across disparate channels.

Key Challenges, Learning Points And Takeaways

- The amount of data available on customer behavior today means it is possible to predict where to find customers more accurately than ever before – and AI is perfectly suited to understanding that data.

- Automated segmentation and targeting of customers can often result in uncovering entire demographics that a business has never considered marketing to, but in fact make great customers.

- Automated marketing campaigns can use test groups to establish the most effective creative approach to hook customers in, then scale it out to millions of others who fit the pattern.

- It can also identify the most effective channels – email, social media, display advertising – and automatically assign resources where probability says they will provide the best return.

- AI-boosted selling is no longer the preserve of the big tech companies, thanks to a new generation of "as-a-service" platforms for targeting and selling to customers.

Notes

1. Statista, Harley-Davidson's worldwide motorcycle retail sales in FY 2016 and FY 2017, by country or region (in units): https://www.statista.com/statistics/252220/worldwide-motorcycle-retail-sales-of-harley-davidson/

2. Harvard Business Review, How Harley-Davidson Used Artificial Intelligence to Increase New York Sales Leads by 2,930%: https://hbr.org/2017/05/how-harley-davidson-used-predictive-analytics-to-increase-new-york-sales-leads-by-2930
3. Albert AI, Artificial Intelligence Marketing: https://albert.ai/artificial-intelligence-marketing/

36
HOPPER

Using Artificial Intelligence To Travel For Less

Hopper is a mobile app-based platform that uses machine learning and huge volumes of historical flight data to predict the best time to buy flights.

Launched in 2015, the company announced in 2017 that it had grown to the point that it was being used to book $1 million worth of flights every day. In 2018, it said that its total sales are quickly approaching $1 billion a year, and it has plans to double its staff in the next year.[1]

What Problem Is Artificial Intelligence Helping To Solve

We've all been there – scanning price comparison sites to find the best price for a holiday flight or weekend getaway, and wondering whether we could save money if we wait another week. At the same time, "fear of missing out" is likely to kick in – telling us that if we do wait, we may very well miss out on the best prices.

It's a problem that's emerged thanks to what was originally supposed to be an efficiency-driving change – the removal of the "middle man" – the knowledgeable travel agent – from the process.

However, it turns out those supposedly surplus-to-requirements middle men (and women) actually played a pretty important role. Their specialist knowledge about the seasonal or day-to-day fluctuations of air fares could often end up saving us money.

How Is Artificial Intelligence Used In Practice?

In effect, what Hopper does is replace the old-fashioned human travel agent with an artificial intelligence (AI) travel agent.

Users tell it where they want to travel to, and give a rough idea of the date, and Hopper gives the best prices it can find. The more flexible the user is about the date or the destination, the bigger the range of flights that Hopper will search, and the more likely it is to find a bargain.

On the face of it this is similar to the way that conventional price comparison sites work, but the difference with Hopper is that the user will also get a prediction. They will be told whether the price is the best they are likely to get, or whether it could benefit them to wait for a better deal to come along in the future.

This may sound strange – in effect, like walking into a shop and being persuaded not to buy yet, but to wait until prices come down. But this predictive model is what gives Hopper its competitive edge over the scores of price comparison sites that also generate revenue from referral fees taken from the airlines it sells tickets for.

What Technology, Tools And Data Were Used?

Hopper built and trained its first predictive algorithms using data bought in from global distribution system operators. Unlike most price comparison sites it purchased historical data, rather than just the latest, up-to-the-minute data.

Because this data was generally considered less valuable, it was able to negotiate a good price.

It then used the data to learn not just what the best prices were likely to be at any given moment, but how it would likely change with the ebb and flow of demand.

In fact, the huge historical database – comprising trillions of flights – is said to be the world's largest structured database of travel information.[2]

More recently, Hopper has started to augment this data with information about its customers. If, for example, they live within close proximity to more than one airport, it will take into account the potential savings that driving a bit further to catch a flight from an airport slightly further from their home could bring.

It may also consider alternative destinations that a user might find equally appealing to their planned destination. For example, if someone is searching for flights to Rome, do they really just want to visit Italy? In the case that this is likely, the user may find suggestions for flights to Milan or Naples mixed in with their results.

Thanks to the speed of the machine learning platform it has built, Hopper's systems are able to make predictions based on its archive of several trillion air fares in around a quarter of a second.

What Were The Results?

As well as the huge increases in the amount of flights it has sold, Hopper has grown to become the fourth most downloaded travel app, after Uber, Lyft and Airbnb, with over 20 million users.[3]

Hopper claims that it is able to predict the cheapest time for its users to buy flights anywhere in the world with 95% accuracy.[4]

It also says that its customers save an average of $50 on every flight booked through its app.[5]

Demonstrating the efficiency of its algorithms for finding alternative start or end points to journeys, in February 2018 Hopper said that 20% of the $500 million it had taken in bookings came from selling flights that customers hadn't even searched for directly.[6]

Key Challenges, Learning Points And Takeaways

- Enabling users to search using vaguer criteria (for example, "two weeks in Australia between May and July") gives customers greater choice and lower prices.

- AI can replace many of the old-fashioned "middle men" roles, such as travel agents, doing the same work at much larger scale and for greatly reduced cost.

- Machine learning predictions can accurately find cheaper flights and reduce the stress and fear of missing out inherent in price comparison site searches.

- Applying machine learning to older, recycled data can generate more value at a fraction of the price than relying entirely on freshly harvested data.

Notes

1. Forbes, Hopper Doubles Its Funding And Sets Sights On The Global Stage: https://www.forbes.com/sites/christiankreznar/2018/10/03/hopper -doubles-its-funding-and-sets-sights-on-the-global-stage/#9061f6a3b39c

2. TechCrunch, Why Travel Startup Hopper, Founded in 2007, Took So Long To "Launch": https://techcrunch.com/2014/01/20/why-travel-startup-hopper-founded-in-2007-took-so-long-to-launch/
3. Forbes, How The Fastest-Growing Flight-Booking App Is Using AI To Predict Your Next Vacation: https://www.forbes.com/sites/kathleenchaykowski/2018/04/10/the-vacation-predictor-how-the-fastest-growing-flight-booking-app-is-using-ai-to-transform-travel-hopper/#76274d8923bd
4. Hopper, Hopper Now Predicts When to Buy the Perfect Flight For You: https://www.hopper.com/corp/announcements/hopper-now-predicts-when-to-buy-the-perfect-flight-for-you
5. Forbes, How The Fastest-Growing Flight-Booking App Is Using AI To Predict Your Next Vacation: https://www.forbes.com/sites/kathleenchaykowski/2018/04/10/the-vacation-predictor-how-the-fastest-growing-flight-booking-app-is-using-ai-to-transform-travel-hopper/#76274d8923bd
6. Fast Company, Most Innovative Companies, Hopper: https://www.fastcompany.com/company/hopper

37
INFERVISION

Using Artificial Intelligence To Detect Cancer And Strokes

Infervision is a Chinese computer vision specialist that has applied its expertise to potentially save millions of lives by making it possible to detect life-threatening diseases far earlier than has previously been possible.

It uses technology similar to that developed by Google, Facebook and other artificial intelligence (AI) pioneers, which can understand and interpret visual data.

The technology, which the company describes as the world's first AI precision healthcare platform, is already in use at hospitals in China and Japan and could soon be rolled out across the world.

What Problem Is Artificial Intelligence Helping To Solve?

Cancer is the leading cause of death in China, and lung cancer in particular is the country's most deadly disease.[1]

Survival rates for most forms of cancer are far higher when it is spotted at an early stage; however, the medical imaging equipment needed to do this is expensive and operating it is a time-consuming process for trained medical technicians.

This means that survival rates in rural areas are often far lower than in cities where equipment and specialists are located.

On top of this, China has a severe shortage of doctors, and radiologists in particular. The country has just 80,000 trained radiologists with the task of examining 1.4 billion radiology scans every year.[2]

How Is Artificial Intelligence Used In Practice?

Infervision uses deep learning to interpret scans, X-rays and other medical data.

Just as Google's image search algorithms will classify a picture by looking for shapes that it can recognize as, for example, cats, dogs or famous world landmarks, Infervision's algorithms look for shapes that warn that cancers could be in the early stages of development in a patient's body.[3]

Even the best human radiologists are susceptible to fatigue and human error when their job involves examining hundreds of images every day. AI never gets tired, and providing it has accurate training data will not make mistakes or misdiagnoses.

Infervision founder and CEO Chen Kuan told me: "What I saw was that a lot of Chinese people, particularly those living outside big cities, do not get to have any regular medical check-ups involving medical imaging.

"So, they often have to wait until they feel something wrong with their body before they go to a big hospital where it can be diagnosed – by then it's often too late to do anything about it.

"So, what we wanted to do is use deep learning to alleviate this huge problem. If we can use it to learn from the past and assist in diagnosing more accurately, we can help solve the problem."

Detecting cancer was the first application of Infervision's technology. Next, Kuan's team turned their attention to tackling another major killer – strokes.

What Technology, Tools And Data Were Used?

The primary source of data is medical image records, specifically patient X-ray and CT scans – Infervision has processed over 100,000 of each type of image.[4]

Infervision uses a supervised deep learning model, which means that it is trained on datasets where the outcome is known. In this case, it means the deep neural networks powering the algorithms are fed medical imagery from patients who had been given a cancer diagnosis. From images of healthy lungs, the system establishes a "normal" baseline – then is able to ring alarm bells when it comes across data that lies outside of the boundaries of what it considers to be normal.

As it processes more data (medical imagery) the algorithms "learn" to become more efficient at spotting cancer at an earlier stage, as they learn more and more about how signs of cancer present themselves.

The fact that the platform is able to use X-ray and CT scan images, rather than just MRI scans, is significant, because they are far cheaper to produce and are available to more people. MRI scans require more expensive machinery and more hours of work by specially trained humans, meaning they are less readily available, particularly in areas that aren't served by major hospitals.

What Were The Results?

The company has announced that it has partnerships with over 200 hospitals around the world and the technology is currently being used to analyze 20,000 scans every day.

Eliot Siegel, chairman of the Radiological Society of North America's Medical Imaging Resource Committee, said: "The application of AI will lead to a real digital shift in traditional medical imaging, requiring AI and people to work together to meet the challenges of the medical industry.

"In the process of lung nodule screening, Infervision is providing pre-emptive solutions that allow doctors to meet patients' needs in a short period of time."[5]

After proving the technology works for detecting lung cancers, Infervision has moved on to apply it to detecting early signs of strokes – another major killer. It is also working on detecting other types of cancer.

Key Challenges, Learning Points And Takeaways

- Computer vision isn't just for fun image searches and marketing – it has the potential to save lives.

- Deep neural networks enable computer algorithms to become increasingly efficient at sorting images according to how far they stray from a "normal" baseline.

- New value can be extracted from old data when cutting-edge technologies such as deep learning are applied to existing datasets – much of the X-ray imagery used to train Infervision's platform was generated during the SARS outbreak of 2003.

- Infervision stresses that its technology is not meant to replace doctors, but rather to enable them to work far more quickly and efficiently than they previously could.

Notes

1. World Atlas, Leading causes of death in China: https://www.worldatlas.com/articles/leading-causes-of-death-in-china.html
2. Forbes, How AI and Deep Learning is now used to Diagnose Cancer: https://www.forbes.com/sites/bernardmarr/2017/05/16/how-ai-and-deep-learning-is-now-used-to-diagnose-cancer/#24e50af6c783
3. Infervision, About Us: http://www.infervision.com/Infer/aboutUS-en
4. TechCrunch, Chinese startup Infervision emerges from stealth with an AI tool for diagnosing lung cancer: https://techcrunch.com/2017/05/08/chinese-startup-infervision-emerges-from-stealth-with-an-ai-tool-for-diagnosing-lung-cancer/
5. Digital Journal, Infervision Reaches 200-Hospital Milestone, Advances Global Medical Imaging Capabilities: http://www.digitaljournal.com/pr/3928429

38
MASTERCARD

Using Artificial Intelligence To Cut Down The "False Declines" That Cost Businesses Billions Each Year

Mastercard processes billions of transactions every year, forming a crucial link between thousands of banks and millions of merchants.

In 2017, it acquired Brighterion to complete its mission of rolling out artificial intelligence (AI) technology across its entire network.

Its aim was to enable automated, machine learning-driven decision making at point of sale, online and offline, to ensure a secure yet smooth shopping experience at the point consumers hand over their card details.

What Problem Is Artificial Intelligence Helping To Solve?

"False declines" occur when a legitimate card transaction is incorrectly declined due to being flagged as suspicious and potentially fraudulent. As well as being inconvenient for customers, who in an increasingly cashless society may be left with no alternative way to pay, they cost US businesses $118 billion per year in lost revenue. This staggering figure is some 13 times higher than the actual cost of the fraud.[1]

These false positives have serious negative consequences for consumers' brand loyalty – Mastercard's research found that one-third of us have stopped shopping at a retailer due to having a payment declined for apparently no good reason.[2]

Although false declines are expensive and inconvenient, using traditional methods of payment verification, based on static rules and datasets, they are somewhat inevitable.

How Is Artificial Intelligence Used In Practice?

Mastercard applies machine learning to the decision scoring system that is executed when a merchant's terminal passes a customer's card details through to Mastercard's issuers' systems for verification at the point of purchase.[3]

This means that the models that are used to decide whether a payment is legitimate are updated in real time, based on data gathered from all of the billions of transactions that Mastercard processes. It works by building up a picture of how a card is used over time, allowing the algorithms to learn what is within normal boundaries of behavior and what could indicate suspicious activity.

Mastercard calls this system Decision Intelligence, and Ajay Bhalla, the company's president of enterprise risk and security, tells me that AI has created a real-time system that helped the business catch billions of dollars' worth of fraud.

What Technology, Tools And Data Were Used?

Decisions are based mainly on logs of transactional data. This includes where a card is used, the volume of transactions carried out, the type of goods and services being purchased and information about the merchant where the card is being used.

It adds in what it knows about fraud trends and patterns around the world – when and where particular types of fraudulent transactions are likely to occur, as well as the types of business that are likely to be targeted.

It also uses anonymized and aggregated personal data relating to the person making the transaction.

Mastercard relies on open source AI solutions for some of its work, although the majority of the heavy lifting is done using its own proprietary algorithms developed in house and by Brightcrion. It relies on both supervised (using labelled data) and unsupervised (unlabelled data) learning techniques for training of its algorithms.

What Were The Results?

Bhalla says that since the rollout of its network-wide AI platform, the organization has increased its success rate at detecting fraud threefold, and the number of false positives has been reduced by roughly 50%.

Key Challenges, Learning Points And Takeaways

- Decisioning based on static datasets using fixed rules is not sufficient for fast, hassle-free fraud verification over a network of Mastercard's scale.

- Datasets and predictive models that update in real time allow for far more accurate predictions about the legitimacy of a transaction, meaning fewer false declines.

- When Mastercard made the decision to implement AI across its entire network, talent acquisition proved to be a challenge. It overcame this by making acquisitions such as Brighterion, bringing their expertise on board.

- Data quality is of utmost importance in initiatives like Mastercard's – inaccurate data would lead to a potentially even greater number of false positives, or fraudulent transactions being incorrectly approved. Both would reduce trust in the network and lead to financial losses. Because the system relies primarily on Mastercard's transactional data, it is considered highly reliable.

Notes

1. Mastercard, MasterCard IQ Series Minimizes False Payment Declines: https://newsroom.mastercard.com/mea/press-releases/mastercard-iq-series-minimizes-false-payment-declines/
2. Mastercard, Decision Intelligence: https://www.flickr.com/photos/mastercardnews/31335572915/sizes/l
3. Mastercard, Mastercard Rolls Out Artificial Intelligence Across its Global Network: https://newsroom.mastercard.com/press-releases/mastercard-rolls-out-artificial-intelligence-across-its-global-network/

39
SALESFORCE

How Artificial Intelligence Helps Businesses Understand Their Customers

Salesforce is one of the world's leading suppliers of customer relationship management (CRM) solutions. Its products and services are built to help businesses grow and track relationships with their customers.

When it was founded in 1999, Salesforce pioneered the concept of software-as-a-service (SaaS) delivered over the internet (now most commonly referred to as "in the cloud").

Rather than selling or licensing software packages for customers to install and run autonomously on their own machines, SaaS providers charge a subscription fee for customers to access software running on their servers.

For vendors, this provides an ongoing revenue stream. For customers, it removes the hassle of having to maintain and update installations and deal with compatibility issues, while generally also lowering initial setup and deployment costs.[1]

With the emergence of cognitive, smart computing platforms as a dominant trend in business IT, it is now using the same cloud delivery model to arm its customers – businesses – with artificial intelligence

(AI), and help them in turn understand and better manage their own customer bases.

What Problem Is Artificial Intelligence Helping To Solve?

Today's businesses face the challenge of maintaining customer relationships across a plethora of channels – from old fashioned mail shots to social media and chatbots, often trying to acquire and retain customers across different parts of the world. This increased complexity, involving multifaceted and fast-changing datasets, is ideal for AI.

The problem, though, is that building an AI infrastructure from the ground up – developing tools, training algorithms and gathering data – can be difficult and expensive.

How Is Artificial Intelligence Used In Practice?

Salesforce offers its business customer its Salesforce Einstein platform, which it calls the world's only comprehensive AI solution for CRM.[2]

Einstein is integrated into Salesforce's Customer Success Platform – the collective name for the various components of its cloud-hosted CRM solution.

Along with other AI-as-a-service providers it aims to put self-learning computing technology in the hands of businesses of just about any size. When Salesforce started working towards this goal, however, it realized that it faced one particularly tricky challenge. Businesses are understandably very protective of their customer data. Even with the promised advances that AI could bring, would they be able to persuade their customers to upload their data to a cloud that wasn't exclusively under their own control?

Crucially, Salesforce's data scientists and engineers were able to come up with a solution that meant they wouldn't have to. They designed their machine learning algorithms to work with metadata rather than the actual data itself.

This means that they automated the data preparation process, using machine learning to label elements of customers' data – for example, by recognizing if a field in their CRM database contained an email or a marketing objective.

This effectively allows customers to run their data through Einstein's predictive machine learning algorithms without the algorithms themselves being able to "see" it.

However, if businesses are happy to allow other companies to benefit from the insights contained in their data, they can "opt out" of these features, meaning their (anonymized) data will be fed into algorithms powering services that use aggregated, pooled data.[3]

Einstein-powered services are available to help customers run many different business processes, including sales and marketing, invoicing and financial planning, community management and customer service.

What Technology, Tools And Data Were Used?

Einstein's training data is all of the information that businesses store relating to their customers, including transactional records and details of customer service interactions.

This also includes data gathered through its cloud enterprise services such as its collaborative working environment Chatter, and its email, calendar apps and social data streams.[4]

Salesforce built a team of 175 data scientists and spent $4 billion acquiring specialist AI businesses, including Metamind, RelateIQ and BeyondCore, as it developed its Einstein technology.[5]

Most recently, it has equipped Einstein with natural language processing technology, giving it the ability to understand its users' voice commands. This means common tasks such as running analytical queries and reviewing CRM objectives can be done without touching a keyboard.[6]

What Were The Results?

With Einstein, Salesforce has effectively positioned itself as the first provider of AI-as-a-service for CRM.

Companies engaging with the service can expect to leverage the power of AI to acquire greater insights into marketing and customer service issues.

In the long term, this should lead to more satisfied customers providing higher lifetime value to the business.

Key Challenges, Learning Points And Takeaways

- Delivering AI-as-a-service has the potential to drive strong economic growth by empowering businesses of any size to take advantage of these powerful tools and technologies.

- Customer relations can effectively be managed in an automated way via machine learning by algorithms that can learn the most effective approaches to marketing and managing relationships with individuals according to the profile they fit.

- Salesforce makes data ownership a unique selling point of their service, meaning that their customers do not have to let their valuable customer data out of their hands to take advantage of its cloud-based services.

Notes

1. CIO, Software as a Service (SaaS) Definition and Solutions: https://www. cio.com/article/2439006/web-services/software-as-a-service–saas–definition-and-solutions.html
2. Salesforce, FAQ: https://www.salesforce.com/uk/products/einstein/faq/
3. Computer World, How Salesforce brought artificial intelligence and machine learning into its products with Einstein: https://www.computer-worlduk.com/cloud-computing/how-salesforce-brought-ai-machine-learning-into-its-platform-of-products-3647570/
4. Computer World, What is Salesforce Einstein? Latest features & pricing: https://www.computerworlduk.com/cloud-computing/what-is-salesforce-einstein-3646520/
5. Computer World, The biggest AI and machine learning acquisitions 2016: From Apple to Google, breaking down the AI acquisition binge: https://www.computerworlduk.com/galleries/it-business/biggest-ai-machine-learning-acquisitions-2016-3645450/
6. Venturebeat, Salesforce announces Einstein Voice, a voice assistant for enterprises: https://venturebeat.com/2018/09/19/salesforce-announces-einstein-voice-a-voice-assistant-for-enterprises/

40
UBER

Using Artificial Intelligence To Do Everything

Uber built its business model around disruptive use of data – pairing public hire drivers with passengers by correlating location data from both parties' smartphones. This meant it could assign drivers to waiting passengers far more quickly than the traditional taxi companies whose business it disrupted so dramatically.

Although it may not seem like it, Uber has been around for nearly 10 years now and in that time it has increasingly invested in artificial intelligence (AI).

In fact, it has been referred to as the first "AI-first" company,[1] meaning that every business function from marketing to the core business function of providing passenger journeys is built on AI.

What Problems Is Artificial Intelligence Helping To Solve?

A major challenge faced by traditional taxi hire businesses is how to efficiently get customers home while incurring a minimum of expense through driver wages and mileage.

They also have to ensure a speedy response when passengers ask for a ride, so as not to lose custom to other companies or public transport providers.

Additionally, drivers (particularly late at night) sometimes face problems themselves because they have to deal with passengers who may be drunk and abusive.

These – along with a whole host of others – are some of the problems that Uber is tackling using AI.

How Is Artificial Intelligence Used In Practice?

Uber uses AI for its core business of despatching drivers to passengers who are waiting to be picked up, and calculating the most efficient routes to get them to their destinations.

It also powers the company's "surge pricing" model, which increases fares when the service is in high demand to encourage more of its drivers to clock in, therefore reducing customer waiting times.

Hotels, airlines and public transport operators have used this technique of balancing customer demand for a long time – which is why flights and hotel rooms are usually more expensive to book at peak times or during holiday periods.

Uber's innovation is to use advanced predictive technology to adjust pricing in real time, meaning it can more efficiently respond to changes in supply and demand.

With passengers increasingly using Uber in both their professional and personal lives, people may find themselves juggling two different accounts with the service, depending on the purpose of their journey.

Uber is using AI to solve this, too. By analyzing the pick-up point and destination as well as the time of day, it attempts to predict whether a journey is for business or pleasure, and if a user has two accounts on their phone, it will automatically suggest which one should be used.[2]

Uber also uses AI in its marketing efforts, using machine learning algorithms to segment customers. It categorizes them according to how likely they are to respond to certain types of promotional advertising, and even understands how the frequency with which they open messages relates to how likely they are to unsubscribe.[3]

A recent patent application reveals that Uber has even developed technology designed to predict whether a customer may be drunk. Although it hasn't publicly stated how it will use this technology, there is speculation that it could be aimed at protecting its drivers from passengers who could possibly be abusive or dangerously intoxicated.

Critics have said that this could amount to discrimination, and put customers in a dangerous situation if drivers decide to decline them service. It could even potentially lead to drivers with nefarious intentions targeting those that the system predicts are likely to be in a vulnerable state. However, Uber has not yet said that it has any plans to roll out this technology.[4] Perhaps this is a good example of a situation where just because something is possible with AI, it doesn't mean it's necessarily a good idea.

Uber uses machine learning within its Uber Eats food delivery platform, too. Here, the idea is to predict as accurately as possible how long it will take a customer's food to arrive. It has to take into account how long a meal will take to prepare, when a driver will be available to go to the restaurant and collect the food, and how long it will take the driver to reach the customer's home.[5]

What Technology, Tools And Data Were Used?

Uber uses GPS data from passengers' and drivers' phones as well as map data to plan routes between pickups and assign drivers to those in need of a ride.

Data gathered from every one of the millions of journeys made is fed back into its learning algorithms with the aim of giving customers more accurate ETAs for their rides, and shortening waiting times.

If a passenger is waiting on a particular street corner, and it is able to calculate that due to traffic restrictions or speed limits there would be a significantly shorter waiting time at a different, nearby location, then it will suggest that the customer move there instead to wait for their vehicle to arrive.[6]

To complete all of these tasks, Uber has built its own machine learning platform called Michelangelo. As well as maintaining the company's data lake where it logs all of its transactional and customer behavior data, it takes care of training and evaluating algorithms, deploying the most efficient models, making predictions and monitoring those predictions to determine their effectiveness.[7]

Uber's patented method of detecting whether passengers are likely to be drunk – Predicting User State Using Machine Learning – uses data, including customer walking patterns, errors made while typing and how they are interacting with the app, and draws inferences by comparing this data with how they usually use it.

Uber's current AI research division, Uber AI Labs, was formed with the proceeds of its acquisition of Geometric Intelligence in 2016. AI Labs conducts research on applications of deep learning and neural networks that go beyond Uber's own business cases.

Recent research topics at Uber AI Labs include subjects as diverse as machine learning techniques for identifying wild animals photographed in the Serengeti for conservation purposes, to developing and open sourcing Pyro, its own AI programming language.[8]

What Were The Results?

Shorter waiting time for rides and more efficiently routed journeys mean improved customer satisfaction, and a higher likelihood that a user will become a regular customer, with a high lifetime value to the business.

The success it has had with machine learning and predictive models means that Uber has been able to efficiently scale from a San Francisco start-up to a worldwide ride hailing network.

Uber claims an 80% success rate at using AI to predict whether a passenger should pay for their ride using their business or personal account.

Key Challenges, Learning Points And Takeaways

- Machine learning algorithms mean that customer wait times and journey times, as well as routes, can be predicted with a high degree of accuracy.

- Uber looks at machine learning as a tool that can be applied to any area of its own business, to generate efficiencies and improve customer experience.

- Uber has emerged as an "AI first" company with the aim of competing with the key players in the global AI revolution, such as Google, Facebook and Amazon.

- Uber's rapid success has disrupted the traditional taxi hire business around the world.

Notes

1. Forbes, Uber Might Be The First AI-First Company, Which Is Why They "Don't Even Think About It Anymore": https://www.forbes.com/sites/johnkoetsier/2018/08/22/uber-might-be-the-first-ai-first-company-which-is-why-they-dont-even-think-about-it-anymore/#49b54a165b62
2. BGR, Uber to use Artificial Intelligence to help differentiate between personal and business rides: https://www.bgr.in/news/uber-to-use-artificial-intelligence-to-help-differentiate-between-personal-and-business-rides/
3. Techwire Asia, How does Uber use AI and ML for marketing?: https://techwireasia.com/2018/06/how-does-uber-use-ai-and-ml-for-marketing/
4. Independent, Uber Patent uses Artificial Intelligence to Tell if You're Drunk: https://www.independent.co.uk/life-style/gadgets-and-tech/news/uber-patent-drunk-passenger-ai-artificial-intelligence-app-a8395086.html
5. Uber Engineering, Meet Michelangelo: Uber's Machine Learning Platform: https://eng.uber.com/michelangelo/
6. Tech Republic, How data and machine learning are "part of Uber's DNA": https://www.techrepublic.com/article/how-data-and-machine-learning-are-part-of-ubers-dna/
7. Uber Engineering, Meet Michelangelo: Uber's Machine Learning Platform: https://eng.uber.com/michelangelo/
8. Uber AI Labs: http://uber.ai/

Part 5
MANUFACTURING, AUTOMOTIVE, AEROSPACE AND INDUSTRY 4.0 COMPANIES

41
BMW

Using Artificial Intelligence To Build And Drive The Cars Of Tomorrow

German automobile manufacturer BMW builds and sells 2.5 million cars every year all around the world, badged with its BMW, Mini and Rolls Royce brands.

With a reputation for excellence and early adoption of new technology, its vehicles are some of the most sophisticated on the roads, and like its rival Daimler, it is a frontrunner in the race to make self-driving cars an everyday reality.

BMW operates more than 30 assembly facilities spread across 15 countries, involving a vast logistics operation in which efficiency is key to remaining profitable and competitive with old rivals such as Daimler and new challengers like Tesla.

What Problems Is Artificial Intelligence Helping To Solve?

Car manufacturing is a hugely costly and labour-intensive industry where millions are spent each year on research and development, production and marketing. This can drive revenues of billions, but mistakes at any stage of the fast-moving, complex process can be extremely costly – particularly if they are not discovered before vehicles hit the roads.

On top of this, more than 100,000 people around the world die in road accidents every year, with the majority caused by driver error. Self-driving cars are being developed as the answer to this needless waste of human life, but first they must be trained to understand how to navigate and interact with other cars, either automated or driven by humans.

How Is Artificial Intelligence Used In Practice?

Like most businesses that are investing in artificial intelligence (AI), there are two main threads to BMW's activities. One is integrating autonomy throughout their own business processes to streamline them, drive efficiency and discover new opportunities. The other is to integrate AI into their products and services to create more compelling offerings for their customers.

Back in 2016, a partnership with IBM saw four BMW i8 vehicles connected to the IBM Watson cognitive computing platform through their Bluemix cloud service. The idea was that the car could learn how to improve its understanding of driver behavior and then adapt its system to suit personal preferences. By uploading all the data it gathers to the cloud, the system is able to build a vast database of user behaviors, and then use machine learning to anticipate the needs and preferences of other drivers.

Following the trial, the system was rolled out to users of BMW's ConnectedDrive app in Germany in 2017. Examples of how it can be used include quicker and more accurate diagnosis of vehicle faults and access to cheaper insurance premiums if drivers are willing to share their data with insurance companies.

Another partnership has seen BMW teaming up with Intel, which recently acquired computer vision specialists Mobileye. Computer vision is essential to cars being able to operate autonomously – essentially it is the process that allows cars to "see" by analyzing image data from onboard cameras and therefore react to the world around it.

This technology uses machine learning to categorize images as they are captured – allowing the car to decide in milliseconds how it should react to objects such as other vehicles or even pedestrians stepping into the road in its path. By analyzing a sequence of images from a video feed, it can not only determine what an object is, but how far away it is, what direction it is travelling in and at what speed. These are all processes that our human brains have learned through evolution to carry out subconsciously. Within limited parameters, humans are very efficient at doing so – however, natural evolution doesn't happen quickly enough to keep pace with the speed of technological progress in a world that has gone from horses and carts to 100 kph motor cars in a little over 100 years. Hence, the large number of casualties caused by underestimating speeds, overestimating distances or simply lack of attention. Computer-driven cars will not make those same errors.

One challenge is that developing autonomous driving systems requires huge amounts of data to train vehicles to tackle every permutation of situations they may come across on the roads. According to Sam Huang, of BMW iVentures, an autonomous system may have to drive around 6 billion miles before it is fully trained.

BMW's solution here is that these miles don't all have to be driven in the "real world". To this end, it is investing €100 million in what it says will be the world's most advanced driving simulation center in Munich, Germany. BMW describes this as "bringing the road into the lab" and it will allow them to gather data for training autonomous vehicles far more quickly, cheaply and safely.

What Were The Results?

Although a few years away from becoming part of our everyday lives, BMW has unveiled several concept models that represent the fruits of its research into AI-assisted cars and autonomous vehicles.

Likely to be mostly of interest to the super-rich is the Rolls Royce concept model 103EX, controlled by an AI known as Eleanor – named after the actress who inspired the marque's famous Spirit of Ecstasy head ornament. In fitting with the brand's image, Eleanor is styled as an AI chauffeur rather than simply an AI assistant as used in other connected cars. The car is even capable of generating a "virtual red carpet" using LED projectors to ensure the occupants always alight in style.

Perhaps of more relevance to most of us, the Mini Vision Next 100 is designed for a future where car sharing is forecast to play an increasing part in our lives. Here, technology is purposed to recognize different drivers as they enter different vehicles in a fleet and adapt to our preferences. It will also autonomously drive to its servicing hub between users, to be cleaned and prepped for the next user.

Autonomous Mini concepts have also been set out, and here the aim is to produce a consumer product that interacts seamlessly with our lives, just as smartphone and other connected device manufacturers hope to do.

For other applications that are likely to enjoy a wider exposure among its customers, BMW has partnered with a number of leaders in the AI field, including IBM. Its Watson cognitive computing platform was used in prototype i8 hybrid vehicles to learn about how drivers and their cars' systems can interact more comfortably and naturally.

Areas where IBM has said that Watson will be put to work are self-diagnosis of faults and issues that are limiting car performance, management of communications with other autonomous cars and detecting and adapting to drivers' preferences.

What Technology, Tools And Data Were Used?

BMW is using computer vision technology created by Intel, through its work with MobilEye, to train autonomous cars to navigate urban and rural roads. It also works with IBM's Watson cognitive computing platform and BlueMix cloud platform to gather and analyze driver data, which includes using Watson's natural language processing abilities to interpret and react to voice commands.

GPS data is provided through the Here location data service, co-owned (along with Volkswagen and Daimler) since its acquisition from Nokia, allowing BMW to understand where and how its vehicles are driven.

Data is collected from onboard cameras, as well as machine data such as braking force applied and use of peripheral systems such as wipers, headlights and airbags.

In its manufacturing and production operations, data is gathered across design, production, logistics, distribution and servicing departments, and here BMW works with Teradata to automate operational decision making. Their systems allow the journey of any part to be tracked from when it is manufactured to when it is fitted to a vehicle and when the vehicle is sold, helping create efficiencies in its logistics and ensure every part is in the right place at the time it is needed. Its production lines operate using predictive maintenance, which means worn machinery parts are replaced before they break down, driving further efficiencies.

Key Challenges, Learning Points And Takeaways

- Self-driving cars are seen by every major automobile manufacturer as the future of personal transportation.

- The autonomous cars of the future will be safer and more efficient thanks to their use of AI to anticipate and react to unexpected circumstances on the road.

- Traditional automobile manufacturers are partnering with tech companies to bring in the expertise needed when it comes to integrating cutting-edge cognitive software with large-scale vehicle production.

- Before autonomous cars are commonplace, we are likely to see far greater integration of AI in manually driven cars in the form of virtual assistant AIs, changing the way we operate and interact with vehicles.

Sources

BMW, Driving Simulation Centre: https://www.press.bmwgroup.com/global/article/detail/T0284380EN/bmw-group-builds-new-driving-simulation-centre-in-munich

Cognilytica, 6 billion miles, Sam Huang: https://www.cognilytica.com/2017/11/15/ai-today-podcast-011-bmw-investing-ai-interview-sam-huang-bmw-iventures/

42
GE

*Using Artificial Intelligence To Build
The Internet Of Energy*

GE was founded by Thomas Edison and today operates globally across the power, manufacturing, healthcare, aviation, oil and gas and financial sectors. Thirty per cent of the world's electricity is supplied by GE Power's turbines and generators.[1]

In many ways, the energy industry has continued to follow the basic pattern set by Edison in the 18th century. The core process involves the generation of electrons that are transmitted one way between their source and destination.

Today, two pressures – the data-driven, digital revolution and the need for a switch to more sustainable sources of energy – have combined to create unique challenges, but also great opportunities.

To meet these challenges and capitalize on these opportunities, GE has spent five years and a billion dollars[2] transforming itself from an industrial company to a software and analytics company, with a focus on building smart, self-learning machines.

What Problem Is Artificial Intelligence Helping To Solve?

The growth of the world population and industry means there is greater demand than ever before for electricity, and that demand is only going to increase as more of the developing world becomes industrialized.

At the same time, environmental concerns mean there is an increasing need to find cleaner, safer and less polluting sources of energy. Wind, solar and tidal energy are expected to play a bigger role in filling our energy needs as time goes on.

Currently, power is often wasted because it is generated inefficiently or because demand has been inaccurately forecast. Increasing or decreasing the power output of a station is a costly process, and factors such as changing weather conditions can cause unexpected surges or slumps in demand.

How Is Artificial Intelligence Used In Practice?

GE is working towards developing what it calls the "digital power plant", which it believes will be the first step towards creating a global "internet of energy".

At GE Power, engineers have leveraged big data, machine learning and predictive analytics to better understand the stresses and demands at work in a modern power station. Implementation of the system allowed one power plant at Chivasso in Italy, which had previously been taken offline due to its inability to respond quickly enough to changing demands, to be brought back online with half the environmental footprint it previously had.[3]

Sensor data from machinery throughout a plant is analyzed by machine learning algorithms, which are able to identify optimum operating parameters or highlight issues that may be causing previously unnoticed inefficiency.

In practice, this means that production can be increased or decreased when changes in demand are anticipated, and faults can be remedied before they become major problems, through predictive maintenance.

What Technology, Tools And Data Were Used?

GE's "internet of energy" is built around their industrial internet platform Predix. It enables GE to take a global overview of energy production at its customers' global network of plants, which include everything from coal, gas and nuclear to wind and solar farms.

A typical plant is equipped with over 10,000 sensors, which monitor every aspect of operation, each generating around 2 TB of data per day.[4] The Predix platform is designed to be able to read sensor data from all machinery in a plant, not just machines manufactured and sold by GE.

GE used this data to pioneer the concept of the "digital twin" – which is a computer simulated copy of any part of their business, accurately showing how it is impacted by real world factors such as increases in demand and changeable weather.

This means that power station operators, such as Exelon, which has installed the Predix system across its US network of power stations,[5] can more accurately forecast factors that might affect operating conditions. For example, by more accurately forecasting the weather, it is able to understand when solar farms will be least effective, and there may be a need to ramp up output at gas-fired plants.

GE Power categorizes these aspects of its "internet of energy" program as "asset performance management".

In addition, artificial intelligence (AI) is utilized in business optimization – using software from Tamr[6] it has applied machine learning to managing its enormous procurement operations. The many divisions of GE purchase hundreds of thousands of items of inventory from a global network of suppliers, previously with little central coordination. By training the system on invoices and purchase records, they are able to avoid over-ordering and ensure cost-efficiency in an environment where multiple departments may all be procuring the same items from different suppliers.

What Were The Results?

GE Power's chief digital officer, Ganesh Bell, told me: "We have seen results like reducing unplanned downtime by 5%, reducing false positives by 75%, reducing operations and maintenance costs by 25% – and these start adding up to meaningful value."

Using the Tamr platform to manage procurement and inventory processes led to a saving of $80 million over three years, according to vice president of technical product management for GE Digital Thread, Emily Galt.

Key Challenges, Learning Points And Takeaways

- The power industry needs to increase its output by around 50% over the next 20 years, while simultaneously cutting its carbon footprint by 50%.[7] Advanced analytics powered by AI has the potential to help with this mission.

- More accurately predicting peaks and troughs in the demand for energy within a geographic region means increased efficiency and less waste.

- Today, just about any machinery can be connected to the cloud and start to generate data. But the real value lies in learning how to interpret that data and draw insights from it. With hugely complex data such as machine logs generated by power station equipment, AI is uniquely capable of doing this.

Notes

1. GE, GE Reports: https://www.ge.com/reports/energy/
2. GE, Waking Up as a Software and Analytics Company: https://www.ge.com/digital/blog/waking-up-software-analytics-company-building-intelligence-machines-systems
3. GE, Breathing new life into old assets: https://www.ge.com/power/case-studies/chivasso#
4. Fool.com, 3 Ways General Electric and Exelon Are Cashing in on Digital: https://www.fool.com/investing/2016/12/22/2-ways-ge-is-making-digital-indispensible.aspx
5. GE, The Internet Of Electricity: GE And Exelon Are Crunching Data Generated By Power Plants: https://www.ge.com/digital/blog/internet-electricity-ge-and-exelon-are-crunching-data-generated-power-plants
6. Fortune, GE Saved Millions by Using This Data Startup's Software: http://fortune.com/2017/05/17/startup-saved-ge-millions/?iid=sr-link2&utm_campaign=GE%20Saves%20Millions
7. Fool.com, 3 Ways General Electric and Exelon Are Cashing in on Digital: https://www.fool.com/investing/2016/12/22/2-ways-ge-is-making-digital-indispensible.aspx

43
JOHN DEERE

Using Artificial Intelligence To Reduce Pesticide Pollution In Agriculture

John Deere was founded by a small-town blacksmith as a toolmaker, and over 150 years later has become one of the world's leading manufacturers and suppliers of agricultural and industrial machinery.

It has always been a technological innovator – investing in gasoline engines to mechanize its farming machinery in the early 20th century, and in GPS technology to begin the march towards automation in the late 1990s.[1]

Over the last decade, John Deere has transformed into more of a technology company – selling data as a service to allow farmers to make better informed decisions when it comes to running their operations. In addition, the company is offering autonomously driving tractors,[2] intelligent sensors and software and even agriculture drones.[3]

What Problem Is Artificial Intelligence Helping To Solve?

The world's population currently sits at around 7.5 billion and is expected to grow to over 9 billion by 2050.[4] Feeding all these hungry mouths is going to require increasing the amount of food we produce by 70%, according to the United Nations Food and Agriculture

Organization. At the same time, due to increasing urbanization, climate change and soil degradation, the amount of land suitable for farming will decrease.

This means that efficient use of the land is critical – which in turn means an increase in the use of fertilizers. However, these bring their own environmental risks, as well as the direct hazards that overexposure can cause for human health.

This means that when they are used, they need to be used as efficiently and accurately as possible.

How Is Artificial Intelligence Used In Practice?

John Deere has developed machine learning technology designed to ensure that where herbicides and pesticides are used, they are used as sparingly as possible.

Not only does this vastly cut down on waste, reducing the energy usage and environmental impact of pesticide production, it means that the impact of pesticides in the areas where they are used can be minimized. This means less pollution of local rivers and waterways from runoff, while also ensuring food production continues at optimum levels.

What Technology, Tools And Data Were Used?

John Deere uses technology developed by Blue River Technology, which it acquired in 2017.[5] It harnesses computer vision techniques to sense where crops are threatened by pests, and control robotic equipment capable of firing accurate blasts of pesticide chemicals at the afflicted crops, while leaving others untouched.

Before being acquired by John Deere, Blue River Technology had built up a vast database of crop photographs. It then used computer vision algorithms to determine which photographs showed crops that were affected by pests and those that were clean or healthy. After being trained on this dataset, farming machinery was equipped with sensors capable of making the same decisions in real time while deployed in the field.

This machinery basically takes its own photographs of crops (in this case, lettuce), compares it with pictures of both healthy and afflicted crops, and makes a decision about which category to put each individual plant into.

Traditionally in large-scale agriculture, decisions as to whether or not crops should be sprayed are taken on a field-by-field basis, resulting in hugely inefficient usage of chemicals, which may have only been needed in a small area. This targeted approach has become known as "precision agriculture" and is only possible thanks to machine learning and computer vision.

This initiative is just the latest in a number of measures taken by John Deere to position itself at the cutting edge of artificial intelligence (AI). It also provides a service known as Farmsight,[6] which allows farmers to make data-driven decisions about where and when crops should be planted. The data is crowd sourced from farmers all over the world and made available via subscription. The system gathers insights based on temperature, soil moisture levels, weather data, sunlight and many other factors to help farmers make decisions such as when and where to plant their crops to gain the highest yields.

What Are The Results?

Willy Pell, director of new technology at Blue River, said that their precision agriculture system has the potential to reduce the amount of pesticides sprayed onto land by farms worldwide by up to 90%.[7] This should lead to less pollution as well as a decreased impact on human and animal health caused by the hazardous chemicals.

It will also mean higher crop yields for farmers, and help solve the challenge of feeding an ever-increasing number of humans with an ever-shrinking amount of available farmland.

Key Challenges, Learning Points And Takeaways

- Advanced AI could provide solutions to the problem of producing enough food for the world's growing population.

- Precision agriculture means a reduction in the amount of harmful chemicals sprayed on crops – increasing efficiency and reducing pollution.

- Automation is not new to farming, but combining automated systems with advanced sensing and decision-making technology is helping to break new ground.

- Challenges include teaching automated systems to recognize the difference between afflicted and healthy crops – this was done by training the systems on vast amounts of photographic data.

Notes

1. Lightreading, John Deere Bets the Farm on AI, IoT: https://www.light reading.com/enterprise-cloud/machine-learning-and-ai/john-deere-bets -the-farm-on-ai-iot/a/d-id/741284
2. NASA, How NASA and John Deere Helped Tractors Drive Themselves: https://www.nasa.gov/feature/directorates/spacetech/spinoff/john_deere
3. Sentera, https://sentera.com/johndeere/

4. United Nations, World Population Prospects: Key Findings: https://esa.
   un.org/unpd/wpp/Publications/Files/WPP2017_KeyFindings.pdf
5. John Deere, Deere to Advance Machine Learning Capabilities in Acquisition of Blue River Technology: https://www.deere.com/en/our-company/
   news-and-announcements/news-releases/2017/corporate/2017sep06-
   blue-river-technology/
6. John Deere, Farmsight: http://www.deere.com/en_US/docs/agriculture/
   farmsight/jdfarmsight_faq.pdf
7. Wired, Why John Deere just spent $305 million on a lettuce farming ro-
   bot: https://www.wired.com/story/why-john-deere-just-spent-dollar305
   -million-on-a-lettuce-farming-robot/

44
KONE

Using Artificial Intelligence To Move Millions Of People Every Day

Finnish-headquartered elevator and escalator engineering and maintenance group KONE are responsible for 1.1 million elevators worldwide.

It considers its mission to be to improve the flow of urban life, and at Heathrow Airport in London alone it is responsible for moving 191,000 people every day using 1,035 escalators, elevators and autowalks.

In 2017, KONE announced an ambitious data-driven program with the target of measuring and analyzing data collected from thousands of pieces of machinery all round the world. The information will be processed with machine learning algorithms and made available to other operators and maintenance businesses.

What Problems Is Artificial Intelligence Helping To Solve?

With so many moving parts across a large number of complicated systems, breakdowns and faulty equipment can mean that thousands of people are affected by delays.

Having to wait until things go wrong before remedies can be put into place leads to further downtime and inefficiency, while replacement parts are sourced and moved to the locations where they are needed.

As well as this, coordinating different people-moving equipment in large buildings is a difficult task. When someone presses an elevator call button, the system has to decide which car is best placed to respond. In many situations this won't be the closest one – which may already be full, or heading in the wrong direction. As this is traditionally handled by non-intelligent machines, it can often mean passengers waiting for longer than necessary.

How Is Artificial Intelligence Used In Practice?

KONE began the process of teaching machines to operate themselves back in the late 1980s, when microprocessor control of elevator systems started to become the norm. Processors were designed to estimate the average number of passengers that would be waiting at each floor and adapt the way they operated predictively.

Today, KONE has connected more than 1 million of its escalators and elevators to the cloud. They are fitted with sensors that can pick up everything from the start and stop times of elevators leaving and arriving at floors, to acceleration, temperature, noise levels and the frequency of vibrations running through cables.

KONE CEO Henrick Ehrnrooth told me: "We are connecting elevators and escalators to the cloud … that means we're connecting a lot of data, and this enables us to provide significant value for our customers.

"When you're managing a building, it's important to have a full understanding of what's going on, all the time – What is happening? How is the equipment performing? How are people moving in the building?"

With all of this data, machine learning algorithms are able to build models that enable correlations and outliers to be determined, which leads to a build-up of the machine's "understanding" of when faults or breakdowns are likely to occur. This means maintenance work can be more efficiently scheduled, and replacement parts are more likely to be in the right place at the right time.

Artificial intelligence also informs the "group control" function of elevator systems, which coordinates the way that multiple elevators operate together – for example, deciding which elevator is best placed to respond to a waiting passenger's press of the call button.

This is done by taking into account the predicted demand and availability of every elevator in the system together, and making decisions on the best way to move everyone efficiently.

KONE packages this data up into a service it calls KONE 24/7 Connected Services and sells it to other operators, enabling them to take advantage of machine learning-driven predictive analytics themselves.

What Technology, Tools And Data Are Used?

KONE launched its 24/7 Connected Services through a partnership that saw it working together with IBM. More specifically, it uses IBM's Watson cognitive computing platform to understand and learn how its machinery is working.

You can actually listen in on the system's conversation at http://machineconversations.kone.com – and experience for yourself what has been described as "both really dull and truly fascinating" interaction between machines.

Data is collected by sensors connected throughout the machinery, and this includes a limited amount of "edge computing", where decisions about which data is or isn't useful are made within the sensors themselves. This helps to reduce the overall data volume by cutting out worthless "noise" at its source.

What Were The Results?

KONE, as well as other engineering and maintenance businesses using the connected system, is able to better understand the operation of its machinery and more accurately predict breakdowns and failures.

This cuts down on wasted time and energy – both on the part of the engineers themselves and the millions of people that rely on its equipment to get them from A to B each day.

On top of this, machinery can operate more efficiently. For example, an elevator can learn how busy it is likely to be at certain times of the day, and adjust the time it waits at each floor to allow passengers to enter. In buildings with multiple elevator systems, their operation can be co-ordinated so they travel more frequently to floors where they are needed, reducing passenger wait time.

Key Challenges, Learning Points And Takeaways

- As buildings – and populations – grow larger, improving the efficiency of systems responsible for moving people around is vital to ensuring the smooth flow of urban life.

- In industrial applications, more data makes it more likely that machines will make accurate predictions – by "crowd sourcing" from its own machinery, KONE ensures that its systems are trained using the best possible real world datasets.

- KONE has leveraged one of the key opportunities offered by the "data age" by becoming a data provider. It is effectively monetizing its own data by packaging and selling it to other organizations. It recognizes that its own data is valuable due to its power to drive change and efficiency.

Sources

Forbes, Internet Of Things And Machine Learning: Ever Wondered What Machines Are Saying To Each Other?: https://www.forbes.com/sites/bernardmarr/2017/02/21/how-ai-and-real-time-machine-data-helps-kone-move-millions-of-people-a-day/#5a69c1365f97

IBM, More than 1 million connected: https://www.ibm.com/watson/stories/kone/

QZ.com, Listen to internet-connected elevators talk about how their day's going: https://qz.com/910593/listen-to-internet-connected-elevators-talk-about-how-their-days-going/

Smart group control systems – AI work in elevators starting in late 80s: https://www.bernardmarr.com/default.asp?contentID=694

45
DAIMLER AG

From Luxury Personal Cars To Passenger Drones

Daimler AG, the German parent company of the Mercedes-Benz as well as Smart car brands, has a long history of building luxury and consumer vehicles, trucks and buses since its predecessor companies merged into Daimler-Benz AG in 1926.

Today, as well as being renowned for its precision-engineered automobiles, it is investing heavily in automation and fourth industrial revolution technology, from its design and production operations to the vehicles themselves.

Machine learning is playing an integral part in every part of this transformation, helping to streamline processes, cut down on waste and remove human error from many equations.

What Problems Is Artificial Intelligence Helping To Solve?

Mercedes-Benz is using artificial intelligence (AI) to create efficiencies in vehicle production, transportation and passenger transport.

Vehicle design and manufacture is a labor intensive and costly process, involving high-tech plants and equipment and large workforces.

Equipment breakdown and human error can lead to wasted resources, costly delays and injury.

In addition, the changing ways that we are using personal transport is leading to problems for car manufacturers that are sticking to traditional models. Particularly in cities and urban areas, a move away from car ownership and towards ride sharing and public transport means a declining customer base. Often this is driven by an increased awareness of environmental issues, as well as changing urban landscapes that are becoming less friendly to owners and operators of personal vehicles.

How Is Artificial Intelligence Used In Practice?

Daimler Trucks has unveiled the Future Truck 2025 – which it claims is the world's first self-driving heavy goods vehicle. Although it still contains a cabin to transport a crew (who may be required for loading and unloading of cargo) it can navigate fully autonomously, which the company says will lead to improved road safety and lower fuel costs.

As far as personal vehicles go, Mercedes-Benz is also investing in in-car AI, currently known as MBUX (Mercedes Benz User Experience) to free up drivers from repetitive or distracting tasks while on the road. MBUX can carry out tasks such as predicting a likely destination and automatically engaging navigation systems, and even activate climate controls via indirect commands such as detecting when the driver says "It's hot."

It has also announced its Luxury in Motion car as the future of autonomous driving. Its elegant and spacious interior is designed to feel more like a lounge than the cabin of a vehicle, allowing its executive and VIP passengers to spend their journey productively and arrive at their destination fully refreshed. The concept is to provide a "mobile living space" and reimagine the concept of personal transport.

This focus on automation extends to the design, production and sales of vehicles. Cameras, sensors and Internet of Things technology give the business a real-time overview of its stock and the operating efficiency of its machinery. It means that each vehicle can be built to a customer's specific requirements, while remaining in a mass-production environment. This allows it to offer a feature through its Mercedes-Me app, which it calls Joyful Anticipation – allowing buyers to track the progress of their in-production car as it passes through the assembly line.

On the sales side of the business, Daimler also lets potential customers who spot their dream car on the streets to snap a picture using their Car Detection App. The image will then be analyzed using image recognition algorithms, and the potential customer will be informed of the exact make, model and specifications – as well as where it can be bought in the local area.

Daimler's ideas about how transport will change includes an understanding that we are likely to continue to move away from the concept of individual vehicle ownership in the future. No doubt this thinking is behind its purchase of 60% of the MyTaxi ride-hailing service, as well as the Athlon car leasing business.

Looking to the skies, and further into the future, Daimler has also staked its claim to a share of Dubai's plan to offer the world's first drone taxi service. The company has invested £25 million in Volocopter – the German firm that took Crown Prince Sheikh Handan Bin Mohammed on a five-minute maiden flight above the desert in 2017. Autonomous drones will use machine learning to safely navigate past other air-borne objects and react to changeable weather conditions in-flight.

What Were The Results?

Most of Daimler's AI projects are in pilot or prototype stage and there is little data on how effective they have proven to be so far. However, the company-wide focus on intelligent, self-learning technology shows that Daimler is firmly committed to an autonomous future. Self-driving trucks such as the Future Truck 2025 have the potential to improve safety on the roads, while more high-flying initiatives such as Volocopter could help to relieve congestion on the ground in our gridlocked cities.

What Technology, Tools And Data Were Used?

Daimler partnered with Nvidia to design deep learning-based systems three years ago, and the technology developed here forms the basis of its autonomous driving and AI assistant systems.

Data is gathered from the road itself using sensors attached to the vehicle, and is processed through computer vision systems. It is augmented with external data such as GPS and meteorological information.

In its production environments, data is gathered from cameras and sensors fitted to machinery, as well as data from computerized stock control systems, machine data and customer service feedback. 3D printing and virtual reality are also used for design and prototyping.

The Car Detection App uses SAP's Leonardo machine learning platform to analyze pictures of Mercedes cars and tell the sender its make and model, as well as where it can be bought locally.

Key Challenges, Learning Points
And Takeaways

- As with other auto manufacturers, and leading businesses in many other industries, Mercedes is moving away from its traditional background as a car maker and positioning itself as a data-driven technology company. In the near future its competitors are just as likely to be Google and Apple as BMW or Toyota.

- Businesses that lead the way in AI and automation aren't limiting themselves to individual use cases. Technology can be implemented right through a company, from design and prototyping to sales and servicing.

- Auto manufacturers are moving away from identical production lines and building the capability to produce bespoke products with the same efficiency as they can with mass-production. AI enables them to cope with the inherent logistical challenges.

- Automobile production lines of the near future will be safer, faster and more efficient, thanks to an improved ability to collect and analyze data at every step of the process.

Sources

Business Insider, MBUX: http://uk.businessinsider.com/mercedes-building-its-own-ai-powered-voice-assistant-for-the-car-2018–1?r= US&IR=T

Daimler, AI in car production and manufacturing: https://www. daimler.com/innovation/case/connectivity/industry-4–0.html

SAP, Car spotting app using SAP tech: https://news.sap.com/2018/06/ machine-learning-makes-mercedes-benz-dream-car-a-reality/

46
NASA

Using Artificial Intelligence To Explore Space And Distant Worlds

NASA will launch its next mission to Mars in 2020. It has landed four Mars rover craft on the surface of the red planet so far, starting with the first successful landing of Sojourner in 1997. The most recent landing was by the rover Curiosity in 2011. As artificial intelligence (AI) technology is far more advanced than at the time the last rover was launched, the as-yet unnamed Mars 2020 rover craft will be the most automated and intelligent yet. Its primary goal will be searching for signs that the red planet may once have been home to life.

Beyond this, NASA's deep space probes – such as the New Horizons mission to Pluto and the Voyager missions to the outer reaches of the solar system – have travelled further than any other man-made object from Earth, and continue to send back data, adding to our understanding of the universe we live in.

What Problem Is Artificial Intelligence Helping To Solve?

One of the biggest obstacles in space exploration is the limited amount of bandwidth available for sending information back to Earth. Due to the distances involved, even today these data volumes are measured in mere megabits.

Particularly when exploring the far reaches of the solar system, unmanned spacecraft can often be out of contact with humans for long periods of time. Their ability to make autonomous decisions about what information is valuable to their Earth-bound operators is vital.

Another problem is the limited amount of power available to operate the spacecraft. As they are often far from recharging stations, and even further from the sun's source of solar energy, power usage must be carefully predicted and monitored. Running out of energy on the surface of a distant planet or in the far reaches of interplanetary space means a multi-billion dollar spacecraft becomes a non-responsive and inoperative hunk of metal, plastic and circuitry.

Additionally, when it comes to manned space exploration, problems arise because working conditions in space often put stresses on the human body far beyond those that human bodies are used to coping with.

How Is Artificial Intelligence Used In Practice?

Spacecraft – from deep space probes to planetary landers like the rovers – are equipped with a large number of sensors to capture every possible piece of information about the environments. This isn't because most of that information is useful – in fact, it generally isn't. The vast majority of space is an empty vacuum and the vast majority of planetary surfaces are comprised of lifeless, inert matter, no different from that found on Earth.

Instead, what it is used for is to build an understanding of what is normal, so that interesting, unusual and valuable information stands out. Teaching space-faring machines to recognize this anomalous data is the main purpose of AI work carried out by NASA.

As Kiri Wagstaff, principal data scientist with NASA's Jet Propulsion Laboratory machine learning group, says: "We don't want to miss something just because we didn't know to look for it.

"We want the spacecraft to know what we expect to see and recognize when it observes something different. If you know a lot in advance you can build a model of normality – of what the robots should expect to see. For new environments we want to let the spacecraft build a model of normality based on its own observations, that way it can recognize surprises we haven't anticipated."

Smart systems also carefully monitor the power usage of spacecraft – particularly the Mars rovers – to determine which systems are using the most energy, and what can be shut down at any given time to ease the burden on the radioisotope thermoelectric and solar generators. Data on energy use can be correlated in real time with the craft's "plans" for what it has to do over a particular time period – travelling or taking readings – to ensure that the 100 watts of power available at any time are used efficiently.

AI-driven robots are also increasingly being used to augment the abilities of human astronauts working in space. Since the 1970s, NASA has been developing humanoid robots that can carry out manual work or provide assistance alongside human crews. NASA currently uses a robotic system known as Robonaut 2 to assist humans carrying out complex technical operations in the hazardous environments of outer space. Robonaut 2 is a modular, humanoid robot equipped with AI-driven image recognition technology.

What Were The Results?

Previous rover missions, which did not rely on autonomous decision making by onboard systems, were constrained by the fact that it took 24 minutes for information gathered by their sensors to reach Earth, and another 24 minutes for instructions based on that information to be returned to the red planet. For deep space probes, that delay is obviously far longer. Thanks to the implementation of AI systems, information can now be acted on almost instantaneously by the rover, meaning it can make up its own mind about which locations are worth investigating. Given the huge cost of operating interplanetary vehicles and their Earth-bound operation centers, this means more productive missions and a greater human understanding of what lies on the "final frontier".

The smart data-driven analytics engines on board the Curiosity rover were instrumental in helping NASA establish that Mars once was a habitable environment for life. The next rover – scheduled to launch in 2020 – will be built around this technology from the ground up, and its mission will be to find out whether life actually existed on Mars.

What Technology, Tools And Data Were Used?

To sift through the vast amounts of data collected by lander craft and probes, NASA relies on similar tools to those used by today's data-driven online services such as Netflix and Amazon.

Elasticsearch – the open source search and analytics engine – forms the backbone of several AI systems, including those used on the rover but also to capture high-resolution data on soil moisture across wide geographical areas back home on Earth.

It also uses a software system called AEGIS (Autonomous Exploration for Gathering Advanced Science) to determine interesting features such as anomalous rocks that can be vaporized by Curiosity's lasers so that their composition can be determined.

Robonaut 2 was developed in cooperation with General Motors and has almost human levels of manual dexterity. It became the first humanoid robot in space when it was despatched to the International Space Station in 2011. Since then it has received continual upgrades and is currently capable of carrying out many manual, repetitive and dangerous tasks. In the future, it is planned that it could lead the way on missions to other planets such as Mars, with the task of preparing environments suitable for arriving humans. The technology is also available for licensing by other companies, and NASA points to its suitability in a wide range of logistics, manufacturing, industrial and medical roles.

Key Challenges, Learning Points And Takeaways

- NASA is pioneering AI to help solve problems in outer space as well as back home on Earth.

- Space exploration generates huge volumes of data, and it is far more efficient to use autonomous machines to work out what is worth sending home and what can be discarded.

- Technology developed for space exploration often has utilities back home on Earth and licensing them can help fund the high cost of development and deployment in space.

Sources

NASA, A.I. Will Prepare Robots for the Unknown: https://mars.nasa.gov/news/2884/ai-will-prepare-robots-for-the-unknown/

NASA, Towards Autonomous Operation of Robonaut 2, Julia M. Badger, Stephen W. Hart and J.D. Yamokoski: https://ntrs.nasa.gov/archive/nasa/casi.ntrs.nasa.gov/20110024047.pdf

NASA, Robonaut 2 Technology Suite Offers Opportunities in Vast Range of Industries: https://robonaut.jsc.nasa.gov/R2/

47
SHELL

Using Artificial Intelligence To Tackle The Energy Transition

Royal Dutch Shell started out as a shop selling seashells and is, as of 2018, the world's fifth largest company by revenue.[1] Its activities span the whole fuel supply chain from exploration and drilling to refining and retail. Shell is a world leader of end-to-end fuel production – exploration, mining, refinery and retail – including oil, gas, biofuel, wind and solar.

A major challenge it is facing right now is energy transition – the move away from fossil fuels towards cleaner sources of energy. However, it maintains that renewables cannot yet supply all of the energy needed by us to function at our current level of activity and comfort.

Striving to deploy artificial intelligence (AI) throughout its business means covering both of these positions. Therefore, Shell investigates smart technological solutions to both fossil fuel mining to drive efficiencies, which in itself cuts emissions, and to its objectives in renewables.

What Problem Is Artificial Intelligence Helping To Solve?

Experts agree that the future of driving is likely to be electric, and reconsidering our relationship with the internal combustion engine has a big part to play in hitting climate change targets.

But one of the reasons most commonly given by drivers for delaying the change is due to a lack of roadside charging facilities.[2]

Shell is working to increase its RechargePlus charging stations but the "rush-hour" pattern of driving behavior, particularly in cities, is problematic.

As Daniel Jeavons, general manager for data science at Shell, told me: "If you think about it, as a grid operator you're operating many, many electric charging posts … if all the cars all plug in at the same time and automatically start charging, you create a big load on the grid … which, by the way, can't be filled by solar, because it's 7 am or 8 am in the morning."

This means that the grid supplying the charging stations will have no choice but to use energy generated from fossil fuels to provide your electricity, somewhat negating the good you are doing the planet by driving electric in the first place!

How Is Artificial Intelligence Used In Practice?

Shell's system, which it leases to electric vehicle charging site owners, uses AI to power analytics, which can spread the load caused by rush-hour demand for charging.

By getting to understand the patterns in the peaks and troughs of customers using the charge points, it builds up a profile that can be used to predict energy demand.

This effectively allows the charging point network to stagger the use of energy through the day, ensuring power is always available when it is needed, and it isn't wastefully generated at times when it isn't.

Jeavons says: "So what we can do by understanding people's charge profiles is we can spread the load during the day, which basically means we can save the consumer money. But also more renewables are used – because if you can charge more people at lunchtime, there's going to be more solar on the grid at that point.

"It's an example of where we see the role of artificial intelligence playing a key part – thinking about not just how we can make things more efficient, but also how we can change energy consumption patterns to take more advantage of renewable sources."

What Technology, Tools And Data Were Used?

Shell supplies the entire end-to-end network used by the charging points. This includes generating the power itself, installing and monitoring the charging stations, processing data in the cloud, and developing and supporting the app used by drivers to interface with the system.

This means that it is able to collect data on every step of the process. The app drivers use to control the charge also allows Shell to profile drivers to understand how demand changes around the day at its charging points.

Power cost savings generated by the cuts in wastage can be passed back either to the customer by reducing the cost of the charge or to the site owner (depending on the owner's business model).

What Were The Results?

So far, Shell's RechargePlus has been rolled out in California, where results will be monitored before the technology is rolled out in other territories.

Although there are no concrete results published yet, the experience it has given Shell with rolling out AI technology is likely to prove very valuable when it comes to planning further deployments.

Jeavons says: "What it means in practice is that we as a data science team are in a great position, because we can make our current business more effective, more efficient, more reliable, safer – by applying AI into those settings – and that's great.

"But we can also play a role in creating some of the new business models that we want to create and that's really exciting, because we're playing our part in taking Shell into the next generation of energy sources, new fuels, and new sources of revenue."

Key Challenges, Learning Points And Takeaways

- Shell employs AI solutions across its business with key use cases around meeting its energy transition targets.

- Drivers often cite a lack of available charging infrastructure as a reason for continuing to choose fossil fuel-powered vehicles.

- Charging site owners don't like to front the cost of installing infrastructure before the user base is in place – but supplying infrastructure-as-a-demand helps them to share some of the risk with Shell.

- AI can be used to understand and predict energy demand at recharging points, and can regulate supply to avoid adding unnecessary strain at peak times.

Notes

1. Fortune, Royal Dutch Shell: http://fortune.com/global500/royal-dutch-shell/
2. Autotrader research published in PV Magazine, UK drivers don't plan on buying an electric car for almost a decade: https://www.pv-magazine.com/press-releases/uk-drivers-dont-plan-on-buying-an-electric-car-for-almost-a-decade/

48
SIEMENS

Using Artificial Intelligence And Analytics
To Build The Internet Of Trains

Siemens AG is a German industrial conglomerate that manufactures and sells transport machinery, medical equipment, water treatment systems and alarm systems, as well as provides financial and consulting services.

In recent years, Siemens has been rolling out its vision for what it calls the "internet of trains". This is the on-rails segment of the wider Internet of Things – the concept that devices of all shapes and sizes can be networked through the cloud and empowered to talk to each other.

With the market for "smart railways" products and services forecast to grow from $11 billion in 2017 to over $27 billion by 2023,[1] Siemens is making its play for its share of the cake with its Railigent predictive artificial intelligence (AI) platform.

What Problems Is Artificial Intelligence Helping To Solve?

All over the world, time and money are wasted due to delays occurring on public transport networks. If people or goods aren't in the place they're supposed to be at the time they are needed, then business doesn't get done.

Knock-on effects of this include the fact that people often choose more reliable though far more environmentally damaging alternatives – air travel – over rail travel, when they can't risk running late or missing an appointment.

Railway delays can be caused by inefficient scheduling when projected passenger numbers or time taken between departure and arrival are incorrectly forecast, as well as equipment faults and breakdowns.

How Is Artificial Intelligence Used In Practice?

Sensors and cameras are used to measure how every part of the transport system is moving and operating.

This enables a "digital twin" model of a rail system to be built and used to forecast when factors likely to lead to delays or inefficiencies will emerge, and what can be done to either quickly react or prevent them from occurring in the first place.

The insights serve three primary purposes. First, they can improve asset availability by ensuring both that trains are in the right place at the right time, and that breakdowns and faults can be remedied far more quickly by enabling servicing and repairs to be done more efficiently.

Second, they can optimize energy efficiency across the transport network. This means that energy usage can be measured and predictions made about when and where power will be needed. This can reduce the environmental impact of trains – already considered relatively environmentally friendly – even further.

Energy conservation during train travel can be optimized too – with a better understanding of what is going on at a macro level within a railway network, trains have to brake less frequently, conserving energy needed to push them forwards. They can also more reliably travel at higher speeds, leading to shorter journey times.

Third, asset utilization can also be improved. This means more accurately forecasting of the number of passengers, or the amount of freight, that will be transported between destinations in a given time. The fewer train journeys necessary to move all of the passengers or goods, the lower the environmental impact and financial cost to the operator will be.

What Technology, Tools And Data Were Used?

Siemens calls its connected trains platform Railigent, which in turn connects to Mindsphere, its industrial Internet of Things operating system.[2]

Sensors aboard the trains capture everything from engine temperature and rail vibration frequency to the open or closed state of doors, and image data from external cameras is collected and processed to identify factors that can cause delay. In one UK pilot project, 300 sensors were used, generating 1 million sensor log readings over a one-year period.[3] Data collected from the sensors is correlated with breakdown and downtime data.

As well as internal data collected from the train itself, external data such as camera feeds is also used. This allows the trains to capture images of the track ahead, allowing for faults to be automatically recognized and the locations where faults will develop in the future to be more accurately predicted.[4] It also improves worker safety by reducing the need for humans to make manual inspections on active tracks.

The system is designed so that data can either be transmitted from trains in real time using mobile data networks or, for regions with poor coverage, uploaded when a train arrives at its destination.

Siemens worked with Teradata's Aster discovery platform to pull insights from the data generated by the sensors.[5] Data can be relayed to control rooms through a dedicated reporting and visualization platform, or it can be integrated into tools that are already used. Critical reporting and events can also be sent via SMS.[6]

What Were The Results?

As Gerhard Kress, director of mobility data services at Siemens, puts it: "Our customers get more mileage from fewer trains and, therefore, use their assets better while reducing their costs. Additionally, data analytics can speed up the root-cause analysis, reducing labor time."

While working with one German rail operator, Siemens managed to predict every single component failure within the bearings, gearboxes, motors and other mechanical elements.[7]

A critical result is that Siemens now feels so confident in the accuracy of its forecasting that it is able to offer its customers uptime guarantees.

It hopes to improve the efficiency of trains to the point where they can be competitive with airlines, then there will be important environmental gains to be made, too.

Key Challenges, Learning Points And Takeaways

- Reducing delays and minimizing environmental impact are the key drivers to the move towards a smart automated system in rail networks.

- Sensor data can be overlaid with operational data such as break-down and maintenance reports to give a fuller understanding of factors that cause delays when it is used to train AI systems.

- Increasingly, unstructured data such as visual data from camera feeds will be a key ingredient in this mix. Image recognition software helps make sense of this unstructured data by turning it into information that machines can understand and correlate with other data sources.

Notes

1. Gartner, Global Smart Railways Market Research Report – Forecast To 2023: http://garnerinsights.com/Global-Smart-Railways-Market-Research-Report---Forecast-to-2023
2. Siemens, MindSphere – The Internet of Things (IoT) Solution: https://www.siemens.com/global/en/home/products/software/mindsphere.html
3. Teradata, The Internet of Trains: http://asscts.teradata.com/resource Center/downloads/CaseStudies/EB8903.pdf
4. Siemens, Railigent® – the solution to manage assets smarter: https://www.siemens.com/global/en/home/products/mobility/rail-solutions/services/digital-services/railigent.html
5. Teradata, The Internet of Trains: http://assets.teradata.com/resource Center/downloads/CaseStudies/EB8903.pdf
6. Siemens – The Internet of Trains 2.0
7. Forbes, How Siemens Is Using Big Data And IoT To Build The Internet Of Trains: https://www.forbes.com/sites/bernardmarr/2017/05/30/how-siemens-is-using-big-data-and-iot-to-build-the-internet-of-trains

49
TESLA

*Using Artificial Intelligence To Build
Intelligent Cars*

Tesla is a pioneer in the development and marketing of electric cars. It also has a large stake in the future of autonomous vehicles – in fact every Tesla ever produced has the potential one day to become self-driving through software upgrades. It also manufactures and sells advanced batteries and solar panels.

Autonomy in cars is graded on a scale from one to five. Features such as adaptive cruise control and automated parking systems are classed as level 1, while fully autonomous vehicles, capable of driving anywhere on- or off-road with no driver intervention, are classed as level 5.

Tesla's founder and CEO, Elon Musk, has said that he believed his company's vehicles will achieve full (level 5) autonomy in 2019.

What Problems Is Artificial Intelligence Helping To Solve?

Driving requires human beings to be consistently at a high level of awareness for long periods of time. As the behavior of other drivers on the road, as well as circumstances such as the weather and road conditions, can be highly erratic and unpredictable, it's no surprise that over 40,000 people were killed in road accidents in the United States alone in 2017.

Of course, minor (not causing fatality or serious injury) accidents happen far more regularly – leading to a huge waste of resources and time.

And even if you don't have an accident, time spent driving is time that could be spent doing other things – whether being productive in a work capacity, spending quality time with co-passengers or friends and family who aren't present, through social media, or just catching up on sleep!

How Is Artificial Intelligence Used In Practice?

When it comes to self-driving vehicles, artificial intelligence (AI) is used to make decisions based on road conditions around the vehicle, such as the direction it is travelling, the planned destination and the behavior of other traffic in the vicinity. Camera data is processed using computer vision technology to allow the car to understand what it is "seeing" and react accordingly.

This operates at three levels – internal (information gathered and processed internally by the car), global (information gathered across an entire fleet of autonomous vehicles and shared between them) and local (information gathered by "ad hoc" networks of autonomous vehicles within close proximity to each other). When autonomous cars are commonplace, this is likely to be supplemented by data from networks formed between other machines – such as traffic cameras, roadside sensors and even pedestrians' mobile phones.

Tesla's current level 2 autonomous driving system – known as Autopilot – allows the car to match speeds to traffic conditions, change lanes on a motorway, transition from one road to another, self-park and be "summoned" to and from a parking location. However, drivers must remain fully engaged with the vehicle and be ready to take over control at any moment.

AI in cars poses some important ethical questions that have not yet been fully resolved. For example, how should an autonomous car react when given the choice of hitting a small child who has fallen over in the road, and taking evasive action such as driving off a road, potentially harming the driver or other people? A human in the same position would be forced to make the same choice, of course – with no more guarantee that they would make the "correct" decision than a robot would. It could be argued that, given enough data – which unfortunately would require a few "incorrect" decisions before it could be gathered – an automated car would be able to calculate the least catastrophic scenario and take action more reliably than a human.

In the more immediate future, Tesla is believed to be working on a Siri-style AI assistant that can communicate with drivers vocally while we still have to pilot our vehicles ourselves.

Responding to a question on Twitter, Musk stated in early 2018 that soon Tesla drivers would be able to do "pretty much anything" through voice controls. This implies that AI will be used to interpret commands using natural language processing technology for the car to understand what a driver means when they use a particular phrase.

What Are The Results?

Tesla says that its Autopilot system can cut accidents by 40%. This figure has come under scrutiny with some commentators saying there isn't enough data available to prove that it's correct, and that it hasn't been independently verified. In response, Tesla has stated that it will begin reporting its safety and accident data quarterly. So far there have been two fatal accidents involving Teslas using Autopilot, and the US National Highways Transport Safety Administration says there is still "no clear evidence" of an increase in safety.

However, Tesla reports that before its Autopilot system was activated, the rate of airbag deployment was 1.3 per million miles driven. Following its activation, that rate fell to 0.8.

What Technology, Tools And Data Were Used?

Just as information informs and trains human intelligence, data is the lifeblood of AI. Tesla's fleet of electric vehicles is equipped with an extensive array of sensors. These include cameras scanning the road, atmospheric sensors for monitoring weather conditions and even steering wheel sensors to understand how drivers use their hands while operating the vehicles.

All of this data is processed via machine learning algorithms to understand what is relevant to the car's operation, and how best the car should act or react to any given circumstance to safely navigate itself from A to B.

The number of Tesla vehicles already deployed on the roads – and constantly gathering and uploading driving data to the cloud – means that Tesla has a head-start on other car makers vying for the lead in the race to develop autonomous vehicles, which are mostly still using prototypes.

Following a partnership with Nvidia to develop the first generation of intelligent driving software, Tesla has now said that it is working on its own AI algorithms internally.

Key Challenges, Learning Points And Takeaways

- The high level of road casualties we see each year shows that human cognitive and motor skills are not ideally suited to the task of piloting one-ton hunks of metal, at speeds exceeding 100 kilometers per hour, in close proximity to hundreds of others attempting to do the same thing. In theory, machines can react far more quickly and safely, and communicate between themselves far more effectively. This has the potential to save many lives.

- Giving cars the ability to "learn" how to safely navigate is dependent on gathering large volumes of data. This can be done under simulated conditions but information gathered from the real world is likely to contribute to a better understanding of reality and therefore be more valuable, though expensive and possibly dangerous to collect.

- There still exists a healthy scepticism in public opinion over the safety of autonomous vehicles. Until there is enough data to effectively counter this, politicians and legislators are likely to be extremely cautious when it comes to creating a legislative framework for their operation.

Sources

CNBC, Traffic deaths edge lower, but 2017 stats paint worrisome picture: https://www.cnbc.com/2018/02/14/traffic-deaths-edge-lower-but-2017-stats-paint-worrisome-picture.html

Wired, Tesla's Favorite Autopilot Safety Stat Just Doesn't Hold Up: https://www.wired.com/story/tesla-autopilot-safety-statistics/

50
VOLVO

Using Machine Learning To Build The World's Safest Cars

Volvo Cars, based in Sweden, has a reputation for producing vehicles with a great record for safety. Recently, it announced that, from 2019, all new models will be either fully electric or hybrid – becoming the first major manufacturer to set a date for the total phase-out of internal combustion engines.

In 2010, Volvo Cars was acquired by Chinese conglomerate Geely Holding Group from the Ford Motor Company, which bought it from parent company AB Volvo in 1999. Like every other major car maker, it is betting heavily on autonomy – Volvo has said it plans to have level 4 autonomous cars on sale by 2021.

What Problems Is Artificial Intelligence Helping To Solve?

Volvo knows that understanding how its cars are used and the conditions they are driven in is key to keeping its reputation as a world leader in terms of safety. And safety is also a key driver in the move towards autonomous, self-driving vehicles.

Additionally, roads in the developed and developing worlds are becoming increasingly congested, and carbon emissions from petrol and diesel vehicles are major contributors to pollution and man-made climate change.

How Is Artificial Intelligence Used In Practice?

From 2015, Volvo conducted predictive, machine learning-driven analytics across petabyte-scale datasets gathered from its connected vehicles. It developed its Early Warning System, which analyzes over 1 million events every week to work out how they are relevant to breakdowns, accidents and failure rates in its vehicles.

In one pilot project, which ran until 2017, 1,000 cars were fitted with sensors to detect driving incidents and monitor conditions. The goal was to gain a better understanding of how vehicles and drivers react when faced with hazardous conditions such as icy roads.

Another focus of the data and analytics strategy is passenger convenience. This means monitoring uses of applications and comfort features to understand what functions drivers are finding useful and what is being underused or ignored. Volvo director of business intelligence, Jan Wassen, told me: "We are looking into what types of applications are being used and we continuously measure this in order for us to understand what it is that customers want us to develop in the future."

What Technology, Tools And Data Were Used?

Data gathered from sensors attached to Volvo cars is uploaded to the Volvo Cloud and also shared with the Swedish highway authorities. Data analytics is carried out in partnership with Teradata.

To develop systems needed for self-driving cars, Volvo has also partnered with Nvidia and Autoliv, the world's largest car safety supplier.

Together with Autoliv, Volvo established Zenuity, a software development group focusing on building autonomous driving systems with an emphasis on safety.

The systems will use deep learning to learn how to recognize and react to objects around the car based on data from cameras and sensors attached to the car. It is programmed to take all of the data gathered by these sensors and construct, in real time, a "situation map", giving the artificial intelligence processors a 360-degree view of the car's environments. It also incorporates GPS and high-resolution map data to plot the most efficient route between destinations. It has been described as a complete software stack for automated driver-assisted systems and automated driving, with inbuilt algorithms for computer vision, sensor fusion, decision making and vehicle control, as well as connectivity with cloud applications. The real-time systems require enormous amounts of compute power, and rather than building their own processing systems in-house, Zenuity relies on high-performance-computer-as-a-service through a partnership with Dell EMC and VMWare.

What Were The Results?

Volvo's commitment to predictive analytics has enabled it to more quickly and accurately understand the faults and errors that can occur within its connected cars. This means that remedies – such as servicing or repair centers – can better anticipate the tasks they will face and their need for replacement stock.

And its ventures into autonomous driving are also bearing fruit with the launch of its Drive Me trial, which will soon see Volvo XC90 SUVs capable of self-driving delivered to trial customers in Gothenburg, Sweden, as well as locations to be announced in China and the United Kingdom. The users will drive the cars manually in everyday conditions, but will also be able to switch them to full autonomous mode on 31 selected miles of the city's roads.

Key Challenges, Learning Points And Takeaways

- Volvo Cars, in line with every other major auto manufacturer, firmly believes that the future of cars lies in autonomy, and deep learning is the key to making it a reality.

- Rather than huge fleets of self-driving vehicles suddenly appearing on our roads, the rollout is likely to be gradual – with vehicles becoming gradually more autonomous before fully self-driving cars become the norm.

- Safety is considered to be one of the key benefits of autonomy in cars – if properly trained they should drastically reduce the number of accidents caused by human error.

Sources

CNBC, Geely's Volvo to go all electric with new models from 2019: https://www.cnbc.com/2017/07/05/geelys-volvo-to-go-all-electric-with-new-models-from-2019.html

Cio, The rubber hits the road with AI implementations: https://www.cio.com/article/3297496/analytics/the-rubber-hits-the-road-with-ai-implementations.html

Motor Authority, Volvo delivers first self-driving cars to families in Drive Me project: https://www.motorauthority.com/news/1108300_volvo-delivers-first-self-driving-cars-to-families-in-drive-me-project

Volvo Cars, Volvo Cars and Autoliv team up with NVIDIA to develop advanced systems for self-driving cars: https://www.media.volvocars.com/global/en-gb/media/pressreleases/209929/volvo-cars-and-autoliv-team-up-with-nvidia-to-develop-advanced-systems-for-self-driving-cars

Part 6
FINAL WORDS AND ARTIFICIAL INTELLIGENCE CHALLENGES

51
FINAL WORDS AND ARTIFICIAL INTELLIGENCE CHALLENGES

We hope that the practical examples of how artificial intelligence (AI) is being used in the real world have given you a solid overview of the current state of the art, as well as inspired you to explore the applications and implications of AI for your own career, business or industry.

We believe that the race is on for everyone to grab the opportunities AI is offering. We also believe that if you don't, then you face a very real risk of being left behind in this AI gold rush. Based on our experience working with many of the world's leading companies, from AI trailblazers, to long established incumbent organizations, to start-ups, there are a few challenges that need to be addressed to make the AI ride as smooth as possible. Let's explore some of the key challenges before we bring this book to an end.

Approach Artificial Intelligence Strategically

Make sure you approach AI strategically and don't apply AI to an outdated business model. You will have seen many examples in this book where AI has enabled businesses to completely reimagine and transform business models or even entire industries. In our advisory work with leading companies and governments, we have seen first-hand how important it is to develop a good AI and data strategy in which you identify the most important business opportunities and challenges AI can help you address. Once you have reached agreement on the AI strategy, it is so much easier to successfully roll out AI that will deliver real business results.

Develop Artificial Intelligence Awareness And Skills

There is a massive lack of AI understanding and a big war for talent. If the people in your organization, from the boardroom to the shop floor, don't understand what AI is and what it could do for your business, then it is unlikely your company will thrive in the fourth industrial revolution. On top of that we are seeing a global shortage of AI talent where the really skilled people command rock-star salaries and are usually snapped up by the AI trailblazers.

The lack of AI talent means many companies are outsourcing their AI projects to consulting companies. Many of the leading consulting companies offer great services around AI but it is important to realize that companies must also boost their in-house skills and capacities. AI will become such an important factor of competition that simply outsourcing it can leave companies vulnerable in the long run. A better model is to focus on developing core skills in-house and then bring in external expertise to boost capacity and ensure you transfer skills and expertise back into your company.

We have been working with businesses and governments to help them boost their AI understanding, data literacy skills and data science capacity, and have experienced the difference this can make. Once people understand the art of the possible and have access to in-house skills to turn ideas into practice, AI will quickly flourish.

Secure The Right Data

Data is the raw material for AI. Better data means better AI algorithms. The companies that have the best data will quickly gain an advantage over their rivals. It is therefore important to treat data as a vital business asset and identify which data your business really needs. Businesses must ensure they have access to the data they need, both in terms of intellectual property rights and in terms of legal and privacy rights. Those businesses that create a data strategy to identify the critical datasets they will need and then make sure they are able to collect and use that data for their own advantage will lay the foundations for their AI success.

Update Your Technology And IT Systems

Successful AI adoption requires modern technology in terms of data storage and processing power. The reason many of the AI trailblazers and AI start-ups are able to move so quickly is because they have the modern AI technology infrastructure in place, which they often built from the ground up. Companies need to be able to collect, store and process data to make the most of AI. Siloed data storage and outdated IT infrastructure are often key barriers for incumbent organizations. The companies that will thrive in the fourth industrial revolution are those that combine modern data clouds with Internet of Things (IoT) and edge computing technology so they can make the most of AI.

Use Artificial Intelligence Ethically

AI gives us tremendous opportunities to do good, but as with all technological innovations, it can be used for good and bad, and can be used well or not so well.

Businesses must ensure they use AI well and to benefit people and society and not to exploit people or use AI against them. There are many ethical questions we still have to answer about AI. For example, when we use AI in autonomous cars, should the algorithms prioritize protecting the passengers over other road users? In an emergency, how would the vehicle decide if it was better to save the life of the passenger or the life of a child waiting at a bus stop? What are the ethics around AI in weapons? We could argue that having autonomous robots, tanks and drones to fight wars would mean fewer casualties among our armed forces, but should we really give AI the power to kill people without human intervention?

Businesses need to address the ethical challenges and ensure their use of AI is as transparent as possible. They also must make sure their AI is free of biases and doesn't discriminate against certain people. Using real world data to train AI can introduce the same biases that plague our human decision making. Microsoft learnt the hard way when their AI Twitter chatbot started to mimic other Twitter users by becoming racist and abusive.[1]

Companies need to ensure their AI is free from biases and discrimination and must put more effort into explaining AI decision making. Deep learning AI can often be black boxes that make decisions we as humans can't understand or trace back. Understanding why a Facebook algorithm served you a Walmart ad over a Target ad might be less important but if AI suggests removing your liver or sending someone to jail, then we need a little more information on how that conclusion was reached.

In 2016, several industry leaders, including Amazon, Apple, Google, IBM and Microsoft, joined together to create Partnership on AI to Benefit People and Society to develop and share best practices, advance public understanding, provide an open platform for discussion and identify aspirational effort in AI for socially beneficial purposes. Today, the partnership has over 80 organizations across 13 countries as their members.

Prepare Yourself For Artificial Intelligence Disruption

AI will have a profound impact on jobs. As with all the previous industrial revolutions, this fourth AI-led revolution will automate many tasks that are today done by people. The difference is that this time it is not just low-skilled jobs and tasks such as taxi drivers and the jobs at supermarket checkouts that are at risk. AI has the potential to take on many jobs and tasks that today are done by highly skilled professionals such as accountants, lawyers and doctors. Even if AI doesn't take away your job, it augments most jobs.

A good way to prepare for this is to break down your own job into tasks that could be automated today or in the near future, and those that AI is unlikely to be able to do. It is then a good idea to focus on the skills where there is less AI competition and where we can provide the uniquely human touch. Skills such as empathy, social communication, critical and strategic thinking, creativity, high dexterity, imagination and visioning are all areas where humans outperform AI.

The AI revolution will also create entirely new jobs and the demand for AI and data science-related skills is likely to skyrocket for the foreseeable future. Machine learning engineers, data scientists, cloud architects, machine vision experts, natural language engineers, IoT architects, data translators, blockchain developers and data security experts are all new jobs that will be in very high demand over the coming years.

AI is going to significantly disrupt the job market and challenge our current ways of working. In the end we are the architects of our future. It is in our hands to create a world we want to live in and one that is better for us as human beings. If we are really honest with ourselves, then we will quickly realize that some of the job tasks AI can alleviate us from are not really tasks human beings should be doing – just think of jobs like putting together tax returns, trawling through massive amounts of legal cases, copying and re-entering data, etc. And we somehow have an obligation to pass tasks to AI if it can do them better and more reliably than humans – think of identifying anomalies in MRI scans to detect cancer, translate documents from English into Chinese, etc.

AI has the potential to make our world a better place, but to get there we need to make the right decisions and address some big challenges and obstacles. With this we would like to pass the baton over to you and hope this book has given you enough inspiration to start your journey.

Connect To Keep The Conversation Going

Finally, please stay in touch and keep the conversation going. We share a lot of content across our social media channels and the www.bernardmarr.com website.

Let us know your thoughts or questions, we are always on the lookout for new case studies for our Forbes column, and please get in touch if you feel we could help your organization along the journey.

Here are some of the ways you can connect:
Website: www.bernardmarr.com
LinkedIn: Bernard Marr
Instagram: Bernard Marr
Twitter: @bernardmarr
Facebook: BernardWMarr
YouTube: BernardMarr
eMail: hello@bernardmarr.com

Notes

1. The Guardian, Tay, Microsoft's AI chatbot, gets a crash course in racism from Twitter: https://www.theguardian.com/technology/2016/mar/24/tay-microsofts-ai-chatbot-gets-a-crash-course-in-racism-from-twitter

ABOUT THE AUTHOR

Bernard Marr is an internationally best-selling author, popular keynote speaker, futurist and strategic business and technology advisor to governments and companies. He helps organizations and their management teams prepare for a new industrial revolution that is fuelled by transformative technologies like artificial intelligence, big data, blockchains and the Internet of Things.

Bernard is a regular contributor to the World Economic Forum, writes a weekly column for *Forbes*, and is a major social media influencer, with LinkedIn ranking among his top five in the world and number one in the United Kingdom. His 1.5 million followers on LinkedIn and strong presence on Facebook, Twitter, YouTube and Instagram give him a platform that allows Bernard to actively engage with millions of people every day.

Bernard has written over 15 books and hundreds of high-profile reports and articles, including the international best-sellers *Data Strategy, Big Data, Big Data in Practice, Big Data for Small Business, Key Business Analytics* and *The Intelligent Company*.

Bernard has worked with or advised many of the world's best-known organizations, including IBM, Microsoft, Google, Walmart, Shell, Cisco, HSBC, Toyota, Vodafone, T-Mobile, the NHS, Walgreens Boots Alliance, the Home Office, the Ministry of Defence, NATO, the United Nations, among many others.

Connect with Bernard on LinkedIn, Twitter (@bernardmarr), Facebook, Instagram and YouTube to take part in an ongoing conversation and head to www.bernardmarr.com for more information and hundreds of free articles, white papers and ebooks.

If you would like to talk to Bernard about any advisory work, speaking engagements or influencer services, please contact him via email at hello@bernardmarr.com

Matt Ward is the research lead at Bernard Marr & Co. Most of his work focuses on research and case study interviews. Matt's work has been instrumental to this book as well as many of Bernard Marr's articles.

ACKNOWLEDGMENTS

I feel extremely lucky to work in a field that is so innovative and fast moving and I feel privileged that I am able to work with companies and government organizations across all sectors and industries on new and better ways to use artificial intelligence (AI) to deliver real value – this work allows me to learn every day and a book like this wouldn't have been possible without it.

I would like to acknowledge the many people who have helped me get to where I am today. All the great individuals in the companies I have worked with who put their trust in me to help them and in return gave me so much new knowledge and experience. I must also thank everyone who has shared their thinking with me, either in person, blog posts, books or any other formats. Thank you for generously sharing all the material I absorb every day! I am also lucky enough to personally know many of the key thinkers and thought leaders in the field of AI and I hope you all know how much I value your inputs and our exchanges.

I would like to thank my research lead Matt Ward for his valuable contribution to this book, as well as my editorial and publishing team for all your help and support. Taking any book from idea to publication is a team effort and I really appreciate your input and help – thank you Annie Knight, Vicki Adang and Julie Kerr.

ACKNOWLEDGMENTS

My biggest acknowledgment goes to my wife, Claire, and our three children, Sophia, James and Oliver, for giving me the inspiration and space to do what I love: learning and sharing ideas that will make our world a better place.

INDEX